THE

SEAT OF GOVERNMENT

OF

THE UNITED STATES.

A REVIEW OF THE DISCUSSIONS, IN CONGRESS AND ELSEWHERE, ON THE SITE AND PLANS OF THE FEDERAL CITY; WITH A SKETCH OF ITS PRESENT POSITION AND PROSPECTS;

ALSO,

REMARKS ON MONUMENTAL STRUCTURES AND THE SMITHSONIAN INSTITUTION.

READ (IN PART) BEFORE THE NEW YORK AND MARYLAND HISTORICAL SOCIETIES.

BY JOSEPH B. VARNUM, JR.

SECOND EDITION,
WITH AN ALPHABETICAL INDEX.

WASHINGTON:
PUBLISHED BY R. FARNHAM.
1854.

THE SEAT OF GOVERNMENT OF THE UNITED STATES.

A REVIEW OF THE DISCUSSIONS, IN CONGRESS AND ELSEWHERE, ON THE SITE AND PLANS OF THE FEDERAL CITY; WITH A SKETCH OF ITS PRESENT POSITION AND PROSPECTS;

ALSO,

REMARKS ON MONUMENTAL STRUCTURES AND THE SMITHSONIAN INSTITUTION.

READ (IN PART) BEFORE THE NEW YORK AND MARYLAND HISTORICAL SOCIETIES.

BY JOSEPH B. VARNUM, Jr.

SECOND EDITION,
WITH AN ALPHABETICAL INDEX.

WASHINGTON:
PUBLISHED BY R. FARNHAM.
1854.

PRINTED BY
J. T. & LEM. TOWERS,
Washington.

PREFACE TO THE FIRST EDITION.

1848.

The following pages comprise an article which was read before the New York Historical Society in January, 1847. It was also read before the Maryland Historical Society, at Baltimore, and an assembly of citizens at Washington. The interest which was manifested on these occasions induced the writer to enlarge the plan, and introduce other matter not strictly coming within the scope of an historical discourse, but believed to be important to a complete view of the subject. He has, however, for the most part, omitted all such details as would more properly belong to a guide-book; or be invested with a local, rather than a general interest. It is believed to be the first attempt which has been made to call attention to the various questions which arise in the selection of a Seat of Government for a Nation. As such, the editor of Hunt's Merchants' Magazine deemed it worthy of insertion in that well-known and valuable periodical; and it is now issued in this form for distribution amongst those friends who have taken an interest in the subject. To Lewis H. Machen, Peter Force, John C. Brent, and Joseph Gales, Esquires, he is under obligations for valuable suggestions and facts. That he may have made some mistakes, is not unlikely; but he will have accomplished his object if he shall succeed in inducing some abler pen to develop the easiest and best way of fulfilling the design proposed in founding the city of Washington.

1854.

Owing to repeated inquiries for this pamphlet, a *Second Edition* is now issued, with some additions and corrections.

In addition to the names mentioned in the last preface, the writer would place that of John Sessford, Esq., as of one to whom he is under obligations, and whose valuable statistical tables, it is to be hoped, may yet be printed in some convenient form for preservation.

THE

SEAT OF GOVERNMENT

OF

THE UNITED STATES.

CHAPTER I.

FALSE IMPRESSIONS PREVAILING IN RELATION TO THE CITY OF WASHINGTON—MR. SOUTHARD'S REMARK, AND ITS APPLICATION—SESSIONS OF CONGRESS, WHERE HELD PRIOR TO 1790—ARTICLE OF THE CONSTITUTION PROVIDING FOR A SEAT OF GOVERNMENT—DISCUSSIONS IN RELATION TO THE PLACE TO BE SELECTED—DISADVANTAGES OF A COMMERCIAL CITY—PROPRIETY OF LAYING OUT A CITY EXPRESSLY FOR THIS PURPOSE—POSITION—INFLUENCE OF THE PROPOSITION FOR FUNDING STATE DEBTS—THE GROWTH OF THE WEST ANTICIPATED WHEN THIS QUESTION WAS DECIDED—DR. PATTERSON'S CALCULATION—MILEAGE—RECENT REMARKS OF SENATORS CALHOUN AND ALLEN ON "A CENTRE OF TERRITORY," AND INFLUENCE OF COMMERCIAL CITIES—CONSTRUCTION OF THE ACT.

NOTWITHSTANDING the number who annually visit Washington on business or pleasure, there are few who rightly understand the relation in which that city stands to the General Government, or appreciate its importance as the only spot where it is practically seen that, for national purposes, we are but one people. There are, it is true, forts, arsenals, and navy-yards scattered over the country, in which all are interested equally, and which awaken our pride, as citizens of the great republic; but each of these is limited to some one object, and a sight of one is a sight of all. It is only at Washington that one sees a whole district of country laid out expressly as a common centre of the nation, and a city planned solely with a view to the gratification of national pride, and for national convenience; the inhabitants of which are under the entire control of Congress, and deprived of the elective franchise, for the express purpose of removing them from the influence of party spirit, and enabling the Government to perform its functions without embarrassment or restraint.

It is the fashion to speak of the Seat of Government as a place of extravagant pretensions, never to be realized; of magnificent distances, dusty streets, and poverty-stricken people, without reference to the circumstances under which this particular spot was selected for the Seat of Government, the objects contemplated in laying out a Federal city, how far those objects have been accomplished, and to what extent any failure on this score is to be ascribed to the inefficient legislation of Congress. There are gross misstatements made every year by those who ought to know better, and the tendency of which is, not only to prejudice the interest of those who reside upon the spot, but to foster a public sentiment which works no small amount of injury to our institutions and country at large. It is that spirit which undervalues every place, however sacred its associations, if not accompanied with the bustle of commerce and manufactures; which confines itself to the present, or, if it looks into the future, only looks with business-like eyes; and which has, in a measure, broken up that feeling of patriotism and sentiment, which gathers around certain hallowed spots, and the cultivation of which, as in the case of popular songs and traditions, has, in every country, proved one of its greatest safeguards.

In one of his reports, the late Senator Southard spoke of Washington as the "only child of the nation;" and the thoughtful visiter who stands on the terrace of the Capitol, and looks upon the scene around him, instead of dwelling with contempt upon the scattered piles of brick and mortar, will, if we mistake not, in view of the circumstances under which it was brought into being, the honored names connected with its foundation, and its identity of interest with the Union, recognise the full force of the expression, and feel a corresponding interest in its present and future position. The subject, too, is fraught with matter of grave reflection to the statesman and philosopher, as illustrative of the influence exerted by a political capital, the principles on which one should be selected, and the expediency of any future change in our own country.

It is, therefore, that we propose to present, as briefly as possible, an outline of the arguments which led to the act for establishing the present Seat of Government, a sketch of the site selected, and the plans adopted for carrying that act into effect, with a view of the present position and future prospects of the city.

The sessions of the old Congress were held, according as the exigencies of the war, or the convenience of members from different sections required, at Philadelphia, Baltimore, Lancaster, York, Princeton, Annapolis, Trenton, and New York. During this time, there appears to have been great anxiety and rivalry amongst the different States, for the honor of having this distinguished body in their midst. New York tendered the town of Kingston for the Seat of Government; Rhode Island, Newport; Maryland, Annapolis; Virginia, Williamsburgh.

On the 21st October, 1783, Congress had been insulted at Philadelphia, by a band of mutineers, which the State authorities were not able to quell. On this occasion they adjourned to Princeton, where they held their sessions in the hall of the college; and it was probably owing to the recent disturbance, that the subject of a permanent Seat of Government was now taken up, and continued to be, at intervals, the subject of discussion up to the formation of the Constitution. We have no register of the debates, but a large number of resolutions were offered, and votes taken. Two of the most prominent propositions will throw some light upon the views as to place and plan which were entertained at that time.

On the 7th October, 1733, on motion of Mr. Gerry, it was resolved that buildings for the use of Congress be erected on or near the banks of the Delaware, or of the Potomac, near Georgetown; *provided*, a suitable district can be procured on one of the rivers aforesaid for a Federal town, that the right of soil, and an exclusive or such other jurisdiction as Congress may direct, shall be vested in the United States.

This, afterwards, underwent various modifications, one of which was to have buildings erected both on the Potomac and Delaware, until, finally, it was repealed on the 26th April, 1784. On the 30th October following, Congress met at Trenton, and the subject was again taken up, and, after a long debate, resulted in the passage of an ordinance, appointing three commissioners with full power to lay out a district not exceeding three, nor less than two miles square, on the banks of either side of the Delaware, not more than eight miles above or below the falls thereof, for a Federal town. They were authorized to purchase soil, and enter into contracts for erecting and completing, in an elegant manner, a Federal house, President's house, and houses for the Secretaries of Foreign Affairs, War, Marine, and Treasury; that, in choosing the situation for the buildings, due regard be had to the accommodation of the States, with lots for houses for the use of their delegates respectively.

At the Congress which met at New York, January 13, 1785, great but unsuccessful efforts were made to substitute the Potomac for the Delaware. The three commissioners were here appointed, but never entered upon their duties; for various delays occurred, and numerous efforts appear to have been made to repeal or alter it.

On May 10, 1787, Mr. Lee, of Virginia, moved the following resolution:

"*Resolved*, That the Board of Treasury take measures for erecting the necessary public buildings, for the accommodation of Congress, at Georgetown, on the Potomac river, so soon as the soil and jurisdiction of the said town are obtained, and that on the completion of the said buildings, Congress adjourn their sessions to the said federal town.

"*Resolved*, That the States of Maryland and Virginia be allowed a credit in the requisition of 1787, or in the arrearages due on past requisitions, for such sums of money as they may respectively furnish towards the erection of said buildings."

This motion was lost. Affirmative: Massachusetts, New York, Virginia, and Georgia. Negative: New Jersey, Pennsylvania, Delaware, Maryland, and North Carolina.

In 1787 the new Constitution was adopted, leaving the resolution for establishing a Seat of the Federal Government on the banks of the Delaware unexecuted. But the discussions which had taken place on this subject, no doubt, had their influence upon the minds of those who framed that part of section 8, art. 1, of the Constitution of the United States, which declares that Congress shall have power to exercise exclusive legislation in all cases whatsoever, over such district (not exceeding ten miles square) as may, by cession of particular States, and the acceptance of Congress, become the Seat of Government of the United States, and to make all laws which may be necessary and proper for carrying into execution the foregoing powers.

By Elliott's Debates, it appears that the article was assented to in the Convention without debate. In the Virginia Convention, some fears were expressed as to the influence to be exerted by a spot so exclusively under the control of Government, under the apprehension that it would be in some measure out of the pale of law, and an asylum for political criminals or violators of State rights; but the clause was finally acceded to without much opposition. New York having appropriated its public buildings to the use of the new Government, Congress met in that city on the 6th April, 1789, a quorum of both Houses appeared and proceeded to business. On the 15th May following, Mr. White, from Virginia, presented to the House of Representatives a resolve of the Legislature of that State, offering to the Federal Government ten miles square of its territory, in any part of that State which Congress may choose, as the Seat of the Federal Government. On the next day, Mr. Seney, of Maryland, submitted an act of that State, offering to the acceptance of Congress, ten miles square of its territory, for the Seat of the Federal Government. Numerous memorials and petitions followed, from citizens of Pennsylvania, New Jersey, and Maryland, for the selection of a site in their respective States.

The question as to the place to be selected for the "ten miles square," came up for discussion in Congress, on the introduction of a resolution by Mr. Thomas Scott, of Pennsylvania, that it would be expedient to select a site which should be "as near as possible the centre of wealth, of population, and of territory." Mr. Lee afterwards moved that "a place as nearly central as a convenient communication with the Atlantic ocean, and an easy access to the western territory will permit, ought to be selected and established as the permanent Seat of Government of the United States."

On the 3d September, 1789, Mr. Goodhue, of Massachusetts, said in debate, that the Eastern and Northern members had made up their minds on the subject, and were of opinion that, on the eastern banks of the Susquehanna, Congress should fix its permanent residence.

On the 5th September, 1789, a resolution passed the House of Representatives, "that the permanent seat of the Government of the United States ought to be at some convenient place on the banks of the Susquehanna, in the State of Pennsylvania."

On the introduction of the bill to carry this resolution into effect, much feeling was manifested by the Southern members, and particularly by the members from Virginia, who earnestly contended that the banks of the Potomac was the most suitable location. Mr. Madison thought if the proceeding of that day had been foreseen by Virginia, that State might not have become a party to the Constitution. The place where the Seat of Government should be fixed, was allowed by every member to be a matter of great importance. "The future tranquillity and well-being of the United States," said Mr. Scott, "depended as much on this, as on any question that ever had or could come before Congress." Mr. Fisher Ames remarked that "every principle of pride, and honor, and even of patriotism, were engaged."

The bill was passed by the House by a vote of ayes thirty-one, noes nineteen. It was amended in the Senate by striking out all that part respecting the Susquehanna, and inserting a clause fixing the permanent Seat of Government at Germantown, Pennsylvania, and also providing that the law should not be carried into effect until the State of Pennsylvania, or individual citizens of the same, should give security to pay one hundred thousand dollars, to be employed in erecting the public buildings. These amendments were agreed to by the House, with an amendment providing that the laws of Pennsylvania should continue in force in said district until Congress should otherwise direct. The bill was then returned to the Senate, and the consideration of the amendment of the House was postponed until the next session. Germantown, therefore, was actually agreed upon by both Houses; but the bill failed on account of a slight amendment.

On the 3d December, 1789, the Legislature of Virginia passed an act, ceding to Congress a district for the location of the Seat of Government in that State; also a resolution directing that law to be transmitted to the General Assembly of Maryland *without delay*, asking the coöperation of that State in the effort to get the Seat of Government fixed on the banks of the Potomac.

The following is the Virginia resolution:

"*Resolved by the General Assembly of Virginia*, That a copy of the foregoing act of the 3d December, 1789, be transmitted to the General Assembly of Maryland without delay; and that it be proposed to said Assembly to unite with this legislature in an application to Congress, *that in case Congress shall deem it expedient to establish the permanent seat* of the Government of the United States on the banks of the Potomac, so as to include the cession of either State, or a part of the cession of both States, *this assembly will pass an act for advancing a sum of money, not exceeding one hundred and twenty thousand dollars*, to the use of the General Government, to be applied, in such manner as Congress shall direct, towards erecting public buildings, the said Assembly of Maryland, on their part, advancing a sum not less than two-fifths of the sum advanced by this State for the like purpose."

On the receipt of the Virginia resolution, the Assembly of Maryland passed a similar resolution, agreeing to cede the necessary territory, and to furnish seventy-two thousand dollars towards the erection of the public buildings.

New York and Pennsylvania had gratuitously furnished "elegant and convenient accommodations" for the use of the Government, during the eleven years that it was located within their respective limits, as appears from the resolutions passed by Congress on its removal. They had offered to continue to do so. New Jersey offered accommodations at Trenton. The citizens of Baltimore, through their representative, proposed to furnish money for the erection of the necessary buildings, in that "town," for the Federal Government.

On the 31st May, 1790, a bill was introduced into the Senate, to determine "the permanent seat of Congress, and the Government of the United States." On the 28th June, this bill being under consideration, memorials were read from citizens of Baltimore, and from inhabitants of Georgetown, for the selection of those places; and a motion being made to insert—"on the river Potomac, at some place between the mouths of the Eastern branch and the Connogocheague, be, and the same is hereby accepted, for the permanent seat of the Government of the United States,"—it passed in the affirmative.

The bill was further amended, as follows:

"*And be it further enacted*, That for defraying the expense of such purchases and buildings, the President of the United States be authorized and requested to *accept grants of money*, and caused to be borrowed a sum not exceeding one hundred thousand dollars, at an interest not exceeding six per cent.," &c.

The debates on the several resolutions and bills, elicited much warmth of feeling, and sectional jealousy. Almost all were agreed that New York was not a suitable place, as not being sufficiently central. There was much division of sentiment as to the relative advantages of Philadelphia and Germantown, in Pennslyvania; Havre de Grace, and a place called Wright's Ferry, on the Susquehanna; Baltimore, on the Patapsco; and Connogocheague, on the Potomac. The two last were about equally balanced for some time in the number of supporters. It was remarked, by one of the members of Maryland, that the people of that State were in the situation of Tantalus, uncertain which to prefer, the Susquehanna or the Potomac. Mr. Carroll strongly advocated the latter. Mr. Seney noticed sundry measures of the Legislature of Maryland, which evinced, he said, their determination to support the pretensions of the Susquehanna. Mr. Smith set forth the advantages of Baltimore, and the fact that its citizens had subscribed $40,000 for public buildings. The South Carolinians offered an apparently whimsical objection to Philadelphia, to wit: the number of Quakers; who, they said, were eternally dogging the Southern members with their schemes of emancipation. Others ridiculed the idea of building palaces in the woods. Mr. Gerry, of Massachusetts, thought it highly unreasonable to fix the Seat of Government in such a position, as to have nine States out of the thirteen to the northward of the place, and adverted to to the sacrifices the Northern States were ready to make in being willing to go as far south as Baltimore. Mr. Page said New York was superior to any place he knew for the orderly and decent behavior of its inhabitants. The motion to insert Baltimore instead of the Potomac, was negatived by a vote of 37 to 23.

We shall at present content ourselves with stating what we have gathered from these debates, from letters and documents, and from conversations with gentlemen who lived in that day, as to the principles laid down by General Washington, Mr. Madison, Mr. Lee, Mr. Carroll, and others, who favored the site that was selected.

First. It was not desirable that the political capital should be in a commercial metropolis.* The Constitution declared that Congress should have power to exercise exclusive legislation, in all cases whatsoever, over the Seat of Government. If it could be supposed that this clause left it optional with Congress to exercise the power or not, there

* See Mr. Madison's letter—Sparks' Washington, vol. 9, p. 551. Mr. Gerry's remarks—Madison Papers, p. 1,219. Mr. Grayson's remarks—Elliott's Debates in Virginia Convention, p. 431.

could be no doubt as to the expediency of exercising it. The provision was suggested by the history of all European capitals, as being essential to bestow dignity and independence on the government. "Without it, not only the public authority might be insulted, and its proceedings be interrupted with impunity, but a dependence of the members of the General Government on the State comprehending the Seat of Government, for protection in the exercise of their duty, might bring on the national councils an imputation of awe or influence, equally dishonorable to the Government, and dissatisfactory to the other members of the confederacy. The consideration has the more weight, as the gradual accumulation of public improvements at the stationary residence of government, would be too great a public pledge to be left in the hands of a single State, and would create so many obstacles to a removal of the government, as still further to abridge its necessary independence."*

A great obstacle to the exercise of the control in a large commercial community, would be found in the mixed character of the population, and the many elements of discord which existed there. It could readily be forseen that, in the midst of a dense and excitable mercantile population, such disturbances would frequently recur in times of high party feeling, or during any period of stagnation in business, when the unemployed multitudes could easily be aroused, by real or imaginary grievances, to overcome all opposition, and stay the operations of government.

To check such influences, would impose upon the country the necessity of maintaining a strong military power at the capital, which it was desirable to avoid, it being no part of our policy to keep on foot a large standing army. Another reason for avoiding a seaport city, would be found in the greater variety and importance of the local objects for which Congress would be called upon to legislate, to the neglect of national affairs; and in the apprehension, then generally entertained, that the local expenditures and influence of the different departments, which, in themselves, could afford no reasonable ground of alarm, might, in connexion with the wealth and power of such a city, operate greatly to the injury of other places. London and Westminster were mentioned as cases in point; though they, unitedly, sent but six members to Parliament, they had more influence in the measures of government, by their commercial importance, than the whole empire besides. It would become a favored city, and the Government funds, largely disbursed there, would give it advantages, in point of

* Federalist.

capital, possessed by few others. A remark of Sir James McIntosh was extensively quoted, "that a great metropolis is to be considered as the heart of a political body—as the focus of its powers and talents—as the direction of public opinion, and, therefore, as a strong bulwark in the cause of freedom, or as a powerful engine in the hands of an oppressor;" and it had come to be considered that one of the surest ways to prevent our capital's becoming the latter, would be to deprive it of the elective franchise. There were obvious reasons why those who lived under the immediate shadow of the Government might exert a greater influence over the country by their votes and opinions, than the same number who lived elsewhere. Many, at a distance, might suppose that those so situated would have a better opportunity to scan the conduct of their rulers; and the result of the election would, on this account, be, by the successful party, heralded from one end of the Union to the other, while, in reality, it would become the seat of all manner of rival factions, in which the officers of Government would mingle, and be tempted and enabled to use the power in their hands for purposes of corruption with more facilities and less fear of detection than if obliged to go abroad and operate in other places. The city should never be branded with the name of any one political party, but be regarded as neutral ground, where all parties might meet, and be received on equal terms by the residents.

There would be excitement enough attendant upon the ordinary business of legislation, without adding thereto the turmoil and strife of popular elections. Now, would any great commercial emporium be willing to give up this privilege, considered by Americans so invaluable, for the sake of having the Government in their midst? Certainly not; nor would it be desirable that they should, since their voice in the public councils would be important. There would necessarily be, in all these places, branches of the Government, such as custom-houses and naval stations, which were quite as much as it was desirable to concentrate in any one commercial community.

Again, in a mercantile population, the great disproportion in fortune, and the heavy demand for land, would render it almost impossible for the officers of Government to live in a style of decent respectability, suitable to their stations, upon the moderate salaries which a regard for economy, and the simplicity of our republican institutions, would seem to require; whereas, in the absence of all other interests but those of persons connected with the Government, the value of the property would adapt itself, in some measure, to the means of the inhabitants, and then our functionaries would be enabled to live in accessible and agreeable quarters, and to appear as well as those around them.

Secondly. It was thought highly expedient that a city should be laid out expressly for this purpose, so that there would be ample provision for all public edifices for centuries to come. It is true that abundance of ground for the public buildings could have been at that time obtained in or about Philadelphia and Baltimore, but they would have then been either all concentrated in one point, and somewhat circumscribed in respect to room, and choice of situation; or, if more scattered, there would be a difficulty in forming that appropriate connection between them which would be essential to unity, and beauty of design; and, after all, it would be a mere suburb to the city.* Besides, a thousand objects might, from time to time, call for the erection of new edifices, which could not at present be anticipated, without keeping vacant for years, at a great loss of interest to the Government, and to the detriment of the city, large tracts of land in the best position, which, in the hands of individuals, would be built upon and improved. On the other hand, in a place that increased chiefly in proportion as the sphere of the executive departments was enlarged, the lots of ground would seldom be available to any individual before they were required for public purposes, and the cost to the Government would be comparatively trifling, while there would be an opportunity to devise a plan expressly for the public accommodation, to which purpose every part of the city would be subservient. The whole should be, as it were, one great building, of which the streets would be the passages; the the public edifices, the halls; and the private ones, the rooms.

It was, at one time, suggested as expedient to require a cession of soil, as well as of jurisdiction, under the idea that the State or States would find it an object to purchase the territory, and present it, for the sake of having the Government in their midst; while, on the other hand the income from the sales of lots, would furnish a fund for the erection of public edifices, and the improvement of the place; but this was pronounced out of the question with regard to places where any considerable population had already collected; to all of which, Mr. Carroll's remarks in regard to Baltimore would apply. "He believed, if Congress were disposed to fix on that town, it would be agreeable to the States; but he did not imagine they would agree to give Government a property to the whole town and the surrounding country. The other parts of the State had never contemplated making Baltimore a compensation for such an immense property."

In selecting a place not previously occupied, the object of the Gov-

---

* See Mr. Smith's remarks in debate, Gales & Seaton's Debates, O. S., vol. 2, p. 960.

ernment would be accomplished whether the States conveyed the soil or not, since the cost of the purchase would be comparatively small.

Thirdly. With respect to position, while a central point should be preferred, "it ought to be a centre uniting convenience with utility; the heart should be so placed as to propel the blood to the extremities, with the most equable and gentle motion."

There is no common centre. Territory has one centre, population another, and wealth a third. The centre of population is variable, and a decision on that point now, might establish a Seat of Government at a very inconvenient place for the next generation. The same remark may be made in this country with regard to territory. With the rapid increase of States, we should find it necessary to remove the capital every fifty years, unless we anticipated the future extent of our country by placing it where it would be, in the meantime, far beyond the centre of population and convenience. A centre of wealth is open to greater objections. The centre of a sea-coast line ought to be regarded because it is more conveniently accessible, has more wealth, and more people, than an equal area of inland country. Being more liable to invasion on that quarter, Government should be near to protect it. It is also the interest of the back country to have the Government near the sea, to inspect and encourage trade, by which their abundant produce will find an export. When the central line between the Northern and Southern extremities was fixed, no person in the Western territory had ever wished anything further than that Congress should establish their seat as far back on this line, as the convenience of maritime commerce would allow.

This centre of a sea-coast line falls between the rivers Potomac and Susquehanna; the place between the Potomac and Eastern Branch would admit of a navy-yard, and was yet so far inland as to be, in some measure, protected from sudden attack. The Potomac, Will's Creek, and Youghogany, could be connected by canal navigation, and, descending the latter, you come to the Monongahela, which meets the Alleghany, and forms the Ohio. Its immediate vicinity to two flourishing inland towns would give it some of the benefits of their prosperity, without the evils before mentioned as incident to a large commercial emporium; since the inland trade would bring into them a different class of population from that which throngs our seaport towns—one accustomed to the institutions of the country, and more disposed to the preservation of good order. This, too, it was thought, would be a security against the place becoming slavishly dependent upon Congress, giving it a healthy trade, but not one which would supercede entirely the advantages derived from the presence of Government.

Such were some of the considerations which led to the passage, by a vote of 32 to 29, on the 16th day of July, 1790, of an act entitled "An act establishing the temporary and permanent Seat of Government of the United States," the first section of which provides "that a district of territory, not exceeding ten miles square, to be located, as hereafter directed, on the river Potomac, at some place between the mouth of the Eastern Branch and Conecogeague,* be, and the same is hereby accepted for the permanent Seat of Government of the United States."

The word "temporary," in the title of the act, refers to Philadelphia, where the Congress were to hold their sessions until 1800; when, as Mr. Wolcott expressed it, they were "to go to the Indian place with the long name on the Potomac."†

By an amendatory act, passed March 3d, 1791, so much of the act as requires the whole district to be located above the mouth of the Eastern Branch is repealed, and the President is authorized to make any part of the territory below the said limit, and above the mouth of Hunting creek, a part of said district, so as to include a convenient part of the Eastern Branch, and of the lands lying on the lower side thereof, and also the town of Alexandria, provided that no public buildings be erected otherwise than on the Maryland side of the Potomac.

Maryland and Virginia had previously, by acts passed in 1788 and 1789, authorized their representatives to make the necessary cessions.

As we have only endeavored to set forth those reasons which were considered general and permanent in their application to the subject, we

* The Conecogeague is a stream in Washington county, Maryland.

†The following piece of doggerel, from one of the papers of the day, exhibits the feeling which pervaded the many communications with which the city papers were then flooded, in relation to the removal of the government from New York, where the council had gone to considerable expense in fitting up the City Hall for the reception of Congress. It stood in Wall street, at the head of Broad, the site of the present Custon House.

THE WAITING GIRL IN NEW YORK, TO HER FRIEND IN PHILADELPHIA.

"Well Nanny, I'm sorry to say since you writ us
The congress and court have determined to quit us.
And for us, my dear Nanny, we're much in a pet,
And hundreds of houses will be to be let.
Our streets that were quite in a way to look clever,
Will now be neglected, and nasty as ever.
Again we must fret at the Dutchified gutters,
And pebble stone pavements, which wear out our trotters.
My master looks dull, and his spirits are sinking,
From morning till night he is smoking and thinking,
Laments the expense of destroying the fort,
And says your great people are all of a sort.
He hopes and he prays they may die in a stall,
If they leave us in debt for Federal Hall.
In fact he would rather saw timber or dig,
Than see them removing to Conecogeague,
Where the houses and kitchens are yet to be framed,
The trees to be felled, and the streets to be named."

have not alluded to one topic, growing out of the politics of the day, which it is well known, had an important effect in hastening a decision on the question, and which infused particular bitterness in the debate. Under the then great object of funding the debt, the Seat of Government would concentrate the public paper; hence, a situation was desirable from which all parts would be equally benefitted by sending forth and circulating Government funds, rather than building up local benefits

The following extract from Mr. Jefferson's Correspondence, shows how the business was managed:*

"The great and trying question (the assumption of the State debts) however, was lost in the House of Representatives. So high were the feuds excited by this subject, that on its rejection, business was suspended. Congress met and adjourned from day to day without doing anything, the parties being too much out of temper to do business together. The Eastern members particularly, who, with Smith from South Carolina, were the principal gamblers in these scenes, threatened *secession and dissolution.* Hamilton was in despair. As I was going to the President's one day, I met him in the street. He walked me backwards and forwards before the President's door for half an hour. He painted pathetically the temper into which the legislature had been wrought; the disgust of those who were called the creditor States; the danger of the secession of their members, and the separation of the States. He observed that the members of the administration ought to act in concert; that though this question was not of my department, yet a common duty should make it a common concern; that the President was the centre on which all administrative questions ultimately rested, and that all of us should rally around him and support, with joint efforts, measures approved by him; and that the question having been lost by a small majority only, it was probable that an appeal from me to the judgment and discretion of some of my friends might effect a change in the vote, and the machine of government now suspended might be again set in motion. I told him that I was really a stranger to the whole subject; that not having yet informed myself of the system of finance adopted, I knew not how far this was a necessary sequence; that undoubtedly, if its rejection endangered a dissolution of our Union at this incipient stage, I should deem that the most unfortunate of all consequences, to avert which, all partial and temporary evils should be yielded. I proposed to him, however, to dine with me the next day, and I would invite another friend or two, bring them into conference together, and I thought it impossible that reasonable men, consulting together coolly, could fail, by some *mutual sacrifices of opinion, to form a compromise* which was to save the Union. The discussion took place. I could take no part in it but an exhortatory one, because I was a stranger to the circumstances which should govern it. But it was finally agreed to, that whatever importance had been attached to the rejection of this proposition, the preservation of the Union and of concord among the States was more important, and that therefore it would be better that the vote of rejection should be rescinded, to effect which, some members should change their votes. But it was observed that this pill would be pecu-

* Memoirs and Corespondence of Jefferson, pages 448, 449, vol. 4.

liarly bitter to the Southern States, and that *some concomitant measure should be adopted to sweeten it a little to them.* There had before been a proposition to fix the Seat of Government either at Philadelphia or at Georgetown, on the Potomac; and it was thought that by giving it to Philadelphia for ten years, and to Georgetown permanently afterwards, this might, as an anodyne, calm in some degree the ferment which might be excited by the other measure alone. So two of the Potomac members (White and Lee, but White with a revulsion of stomach almost convulsive) agreed to change their votes, and Hamilton undertook to carry the other point. In doing this, the influence he had established over the Eastern members, with the agency of Robert Morris, with those of the middle States, effected his side of the agreement, and so the assumption was passed."

Another consideration which led to the decision, was the deference and regard which would thus be paid to the wishes of General Washington, who had, from the first, strongly advocated the site upon the Potomac, and who seems to have formed rather extravagant calculations in relation to the future growth of the city. Some of the opinions which he expresses in his letters, seem to conflict with the views we have given relative to the disadvantages of a commercial city; but it is to be borne in mind that it was chiefly a seaport to which those views have reference; and we have, in this respect, relied mainly on the statements of gentlemen who lived at that time.*

In reviewing the debates on this subject, it is to be remarked that the growth of the Western country was anticipated, and depicted in glowing colors by some of the members of that day. "If," said Mr. Madison, "the calculation be just, that we double in twenty-five years, we shall speedily behold an astonishing mass of people on the Western waters. * * * We see the people moving from the more crowded to the less crowded parts. The swarm does not come from the southern, but from the northern and eastern hives. This will continue to be

---

* The late James A. Hillhouse, and David Daggett, of Connecticut, Senator Robbins, of Rhode Island, and Chancellor Bland, of Maryland, furnished information, directly or indirectly, on the subject.

As will be seen hereafter, Washington's great reliance was on a canal connection with the West.

Mr. Jared Sparks, in a letter to the author, after the publication of the first edition, says "I doubt if the members of Congress generally, in their discussions of this subject, looked forward to a great commercial city at the new Seat of Government. But I am inclined to think that Washington's anticipations were more sanguine than events have justified. He early entertained very large and just ideas of the vast resources of the West, and of the commercial intercourse that must spring up between that region and the Atlantic coast; and he was accustomed to regard the central position of the Potomac as affording the most direct and easy channel of communication. Steamboats and railroads have since changed the face of the world, and have set at defiance all the calculations founded on the old order of things; and especially have they operated on the destiny of the West, and our entire system of internal commerce, in a manner that could not have been possibly forseen in the lifetime of Washington.

the case until every part of America receives its due share of population. If there be any event upon which we may calculate with certainty, I take it that the centre of population will rapidly advance in a south-westerly direction. It must, then, travel from the Susquehanna, if it is now found there—it may even extend beyond the Potomac—but the time will be long first; and, as the Potomac is the great highway of communication between the Atlantic and the Western country, attempts to remove the Seat must be impossible." "I confess," said Mr. Vining, "to the House and to the world, that, viewing this subject in all its circumstances, I am in favor of the Potomac. I wish the Seat of Government to be fixed there, because I think the interest, the honor, and the greatness of the country require it. I look on it as the centre from which those streams are to flow, that are to animate and invigorate the body politic. From thence, it appears to me, that the rays of Government will naturally diverge to the extremities of the Union. I declare that I look on the Western territory in awful and striking point of view. To that region the unpolished sons of earth are flowing from all quarters—men to whom the protection of the laws, and the controlling force of Government, are equally necessary. From this consideration, I conclude that the banks of the Potomac is the proper situation."

It is true that, at the time these remarks were made, the Union comprised but thirteen States; and, probably, no one anticipated that the number of States would double in fifty years, whatever might be the population. But, even at this time, we find that the East is to the West, in point of population, as the West is to the East in point of territory.

The following table, which has been calculated by Dr. Patterson, of the United States Mint, in Philadelphia, singularly confirms Mr. Madison's prophecy:—

Centre of Representative Population of the United States at each Census.

Period.	Places.	Distances, in miles, from Washington.		
		Distance. North.	Distance, E. or W.	Dist. on strait line.
1790	In Baltimore county, Maryland, 13 miles S. of Pennsylvania line, and 17 miles N. of Baltimore	46	22 E.	51
1800	In Carroll county, Maryland, 7 miles S. of Pennsylvania line, and 9 miles N. E. of Westminster	52	9 E.	53
1810	In Adams county, Pennsylvania, 5 miles N. of State line, and 17 miles W. of Gettysburgh	64	30 W.	71
1820	In western part of Morgan county, Virginia, 10 miles W. S. W. of Bath, 1 mile from Potomac, 12 miles S. of Pennsylvania line	47	71 W.	86

Period.	Places.	Distances, in miles, from Washington. Distance. North.	Distance, E. or W.	Dist. on strait line.
1830	In Hampshire county, Virginia, opposite Westernport, Maryland, and 20 miles N. W. of Romney, 16 miles S. of Pennsylvania line........	43	108 W.	117
1840	In Marion county, Virginia, 23 miles S. of Pennsylvania line, 19 miles N. E. of Clarksburgh..	36	160 W.	165

Centre of Total Population in 1840.

1840	In Harrison county, Virginia, 38 miles S. of Pennsylvania line, 5 miles due S. of Clarksburgh..	21	175 W.	177

Note.—The parallel of 40 deg. N. divides the representative population of the United States into two equal parts very nearly, according to the census of 1840.

The average progress westward, during each ten years, has been about thirty-four miles. This average is slightly increasing; and if we set it down at fifty miles, it will require a century to carry this centre five hundred miles west of Washington, or as far as the city of Nashville, Tennessee.

The comparatively small importance which was attached to "the centre of territory," as a criterion by which to select a capital, will strike many with surprise; and it is worthy of observation, that Mr. Madison, in presenting the importance of such a centre in what he thought the most prominent point of view, remarked that, "if it were possible to promulgate our laws by some instantaneous operation, it would be of less consequence where the Government might be placed"—a contingency which now seems to be supplied by the "magic wires" of Morse, which communicate intelligence "not merely with the swiftness of lightning," but "by lightning itself."

In the course of a debate in the United States Senate on the retrocession of Alexandria, Mr. Calhoun remarked "that a moment's attention to the Seats of Government in the different countries of the world would show that they very rarely occupied a central position. They were generally situated on a frontier that was most exposed, near to those places where the armies would be required to be encamped for the protection of the country against invasion. Look over Europe. Where was London situated? Near the southeast frontier. Where was the capital of France? Far from central. Where was the capital of Russia? Upon the frontier; and the same locality will be found to prevail, and very properly so, in regard to capitals throughout the world. And if it were true in general, it was eminently true in respect to our confederation. Our capital had been placed here, very wisely in his judgment, and he believed it would always continue here as long as there was a necessity for a Seat of Government. If it were removed, the change would proceed from some other cause than the necessity of changing it to a more central position. The attendance of members might be found inconvenient and oppressive; but he would here remark that there was a wise provision in the statute book—a provision for the allowance of mileage to members for the expense of travel. As long as that law prevailed, the Representatives of the most distant quarters would stand in as eligible a position as those of the nearest. They ought to be paid in a proportion equal to the square of the distance travelled. It was an error to suppose that the mere extent of the intervening distance should be paid. Greater distance should be paid a higher rate; because distance disturbed all social relations, broke in upon the comforts of families, and robbed them of the enjoyment of home, it should therefore be liberally compensated. He was convinced that no one here, as far as he was individually concerned, desired a removal of the Seat of Government."

Mr. Allen said that the example of the monarchies of Europe was not to be followed by us, for the location of the capital was dependent on the location of their forts and fortifications, and not convenience in other respects.

This was certainly not the case with Russia or Prussia.

The advantages of having the Government near the coast, to protect the commerce of the country, is to be observed by circumstances of daily occurrence. It is probably on the coast that the principal fighting will be done, and it is certainly here that the most sudden assaults will be made requiring immediate action. It is from Europe that our enemies will be most likely to come in time of war, and it is with the States of Europe that, in time of peace, we are likely to have the most complex relations. It is of the highest importance that our legislators and executive officers should be so near the commercial sections of the country as to enter understandingly upon those discussions in which practical knowledge is of the utmost importance; and it is certain that there will be hundreds called into public service, from time to time, whose first impression of the merits of the navy, or the extent of the merchant service, will be formed by actual inspection at our commercial cities; and while the Western agricultural interests are subserved by whatever contributes to enlarged and liberal commercial views, and the protection of the sea-coast, our Western frontier will be sufficiently well defended by Government, though at a distance, the principal enemies we are ever likely to suffer from there, being the Indians, the power of which unfortunate race is daily dwindling away before the good or bad, but inevitable effects of Anglo-Saxon progress.

We think the positions assumed in 1790 will be found to have lost none of their force, but rather to have gained strength by subsequent events. The agricultural sections of the West are constantly swelling in population, but so are the commercial and manufacturing interests increasing in the East. The same interests which were then thought of so much importance to the whole country are increasing in a far greater ratio than was ever anticipated. The population of Virginia is increasing in proportion as its lands are being redeemed under the new methods of cultivation and white labor, and facilities of access to market are furnished. It is true that the number of new States is enlarging; but if the accounts of the Pacific coast can be relied upon, which represent the harbors as very few, and the country mostly barren, the population and commerce on that side of the Rocky Mountains can never bear any proportion to those of the Atlantic coast. With the present rage for annexing new territory, no one can tell where the limits of the country will stop, either at the North or the South; and it is equally difficult to say what point will be, fifty years hence, the centre of the territory, while from the calculations we have given it is almost certain that the centre of the population will be between St. Louis and the coast, at no very great distance from the present capital, to which railroads are pointing in every direction, and which, in the present progress of improvement, it is not perhaps too much to suppose may yet be connected with the Ohio river by a continuous canal.

But we were further told by Mr. Allen, that the location of our Seat of Government in the vicinity of our great commercial cities, gave to those cities a preponderating influence in the proceedings of the Government of at least a hundred to one over the influence excited by a corresponding number of people in the vast interior. "There were no committees of farmers from the banks of the Missouri, the Mississippi, or over the Ohio, entering the lobbies of those halls and endeavoring to influence the legislation of Congress. There was no combination of individuals from the interior delegated to the capital with a view of obtaining the passage of laws, the object of which was to administer to individual wants, instead of the wants of the mass of the nation. There was no such delegation here."

Can it be supposed that the lobbying committees from commercial cities would not follow the Government wherever it went? The interests of commerce enter too widely into all the ramifications of society for mere time and space to prevent those interested in their advancement from laboring assiduously on their behalf wherever the Government may be. Mr. Allen's argument applies equally to the good and the bad projects. The only difference would be that, were the Government placed in the interior, they would have legislators not so well informed on the interests of commerce by the facilities which personal observation would give, and more easily misled by a few interested schemers.

It has been objected that the Eastern States secure to themselves greater benefits in the way of congressional and legislative patronage for office; but we apprehend that this source of jealousy has been greatly overrated. Is it not rather the section of country from which the Executive comes that governs in this matter? But, admitting it to be an evil, it is one which must always exist to a greater or less extent to the injury of different parts of the Union, wherever the Government may be, since, as was remarked in the Congress of 1790, the capital cannot remain for any considerable length of time at the actual centre of the territory, that centre being as variable as the centre of population.

It may be well to allude here to a discussion which has arisen in reference to the powers of Congress to remove the Seat of Government at any future time.

The introduction of the word "*permanent*," in contradistinction to "*temporary*," in the title of the act, has been regarded as significant of the views of Congress and the proprietors, on the subject, viz: that certain powers were given, certain acts required, and Congress, in the execution of this commission, was confined within fixed limits—was to accept a certain specified amount of *territory*, and by the acceptance, and by the act establishing a *permanent* Seat of Government in accordance with the requisitions of the Constitution, bound itself to that instrument, and Virginia, the owners, purchasers, and inhabitants of the district in question, and the people at large, by a positive engagement to make the Metropolis of the Union durable and unchangeable. John C. Brent, Esq., of Washington city, has summed up the principal arguments against the right, as follows:* 1st. The Constitution gave Congress limited powers in the premises, and that body, as a mere agent, is bound by instructions and limitations, and can, under no circumstances, exercise more authority than is given to that effect by the Constitution. 2d. A change of the Seat of Government would be a violation of the implied contract between the Federal Government and the States of Maryland and Virginia, which would never have made the necessary grants, had not permanency been guaranteed by the solemn act of Congress. 3d. The right and reasonable expectations of the original proprietors, the purchasers and inhabitants of this District, would be trifled with and destroyed by such a move towards transferring the Metropolis elsewhere, on the part of Congress.

* Letters on the National Institute. Smithsonian Legacy. The Fine Arts, and other matters connected with the interests of the District of Columbia. Washington: J. & G. S. Gideon.

In the report of a Committee of the House on the 25th February, 1846, on the petition for the retrocession of Alexandria, the first objection is thus answered: "There is no more reason to believe that the power in this case, when once exercised and executed, is exhausted, than in any other of the long list of enumerated powers to which it belongs, and which it is provided Congress 'shall have.' The phraseology of the grant is the same, and as much reason seems to exist for the continuance of the right to exercise this power, as in most of those contained in the list to which we have referred. If this construction be true, when Congress had once fixed the Seat of Government, it could no more be removed, although it should prove to be unsafe from foreign invasion, or so unhealthy as to endanger the lives of the members of the Government, or so located as to be inconsistent with a due regard to the facilities of access to our whole population, or to their convenience; and yet it is manifest that some of these considerations might make the removal of the Seat of Government a matter of necessity. To have excluded the conclusion that the framers of the Constitution had regarded considerations so manifest and reasonable, there must have been terms so precise and accurate as to have left no doubt of their intention to make the act irrevocable when the power was once exercised. As some proof that the framers of the Constitution did not overlook these considerations, we may advert to the fact that Mr. Madison moved to strike out the word 'permanent' from the act establishing the Seat of Government, because the Constitution did not contain it. Nor is this the only difficulty involved by this construction—the same section gives a like power relative to forts and arsenals; and contrary to reason and the usages of Congress, this power, when once exercised, would be thus considered as executed and exhausted.

"It might be replied that this word 'permanent' meant only an indefinite period; that it was designed merely to require the removal to be made by law, and not by resolution of the two Houses; or it might well be said that Congress could not, by contract, part with a power reposed in them by the Constitution for wise purposes; but, in point of fact, the history of the transaction does not sustain this view of the contract."

With regard to the second objection the Committee say: "Neither Virginia or Maryland, by their acts of cession, made the permanence of the Seat of Government a condition of the grant."

The view taken by the States and proprietors is, we think, well expressed in the language of the Supreme Court per Story, Judge.*

* Van Ness and wife *vs.* City of Washington and the United States, 4 Peters p. 280.

"They might, and, indeed, must have placed a just confidence in the Government, that, in founding the city, it would do no act which would obstruct its prosperity or interfere with its great fundamental objects or interests. It could never be supposed that Congress would seek to destroy what its own legislation had created and fostered into being. The city was designed to last in perpetuity, "*capitoli immobile saxum.*"

While the force of these remarks will be generally admitted, we presume that most lawyers will decide that the proprietors could hardly have been warranted in the conclusion that their interests would be consulted in opposition to those of the whole Union, if it should happen that the welfare of the nation imperatively required such a change, and it should be called for by a majority of the people.

They entered into their agreement subject to the risk of such a contingency occurring, in which case the most they could claim would be a right to compensation for the depreciation in the value of property which must ensue. This proposition seems to have been generally admitted in the discussions which took place in Congress on the question of removal after the war of 1812.

In discussing the subject of removal, therefore, we should lay out of view the question of constitutional right, because of the reasons before given, and from the fact that several eminent lawyers and statesmen during the debate on retrocession admitted the right of removal, while strenuously arguing the inexpediency of exercising that right, it is very obvious that the subject is involved in so much doubt as to present no effectual barrier to the movement were its expediency once admitted.

As yet, there has been little manifestation towards such a movement; and almost all will concur in the opinion, that it would be highly impolitic and inexpedient to excite a political storm in the country by agitation of the subject. During the debate before referred to, Mr. Calhoun said the question of the removal of the Seat of Government had been agitated at the Memphis Convention, an assembly consisting of nearly 600 persons, composed almost exclusively of Western and Southern men. When the subject was introduced, it immediately produced a strong sensation; and when the question was put, there was a unanimous "No!" deep and strong. The proposition was rejected with but one dissenting vote.

The necessity or propriety of disfranchising the Seat of Government, is not at first view quite apparent, and has been the subject of some discussion. If we consider the extent to which party feeling was carried in the canvass that immediately preceded Mr. Jefferson's election, when private social relations were, in some instances, almost entirely suspended between families of different political parties, we can feel the force of the reasoning given for this measure, and can realise what a serious evil such a state of things would be at the capital, should it again recur, and be fostered by continual local elections, accompanied with all the excitement and misrepresentation which we now see every four years in the principal cities of the Union, and in the midst of which, it is not too much to suppose that the position of public officers might subject them to annoyance and insult in a thousand ways, even without actual violence. And, from similar experience, it is obvious that the votes of those in the public employ might be directly or indirectly controlled by the Government, so that there would be, in reality, little freedom of choice. Other positions assumed in these discussions will be adverted to in the course of our remarks on the progress of the city.

CHAPTER II.

LETTERS OF WASHINGTON AND JEFFERSON IN RELATION TO TERMS OF PURCHASE—SITE—MR. MUIR'S SPEECH ON LAYING THE CORNER-STONE OF THE DISTRICT—PUBLIC INTEREST IN THE SUBJECT, AND GRAND PROJECTS—NAME OF THE CITY—CORNER-STONE OF THE CAPITOL—JEFFERSON'S VIEWS IN REGARD TO THE PLAN—MAJOR L'ENFANT: HIS PLAN, ITS DEFECTS AND MERITS—REASON FOR PLACING PUBLIC BUILDINGS AT A DISTANCE FROM EACH OTHER—THE MALL—RESIDENCE FOR FOREIGN MINISTERS—DIMENSIONS OF THE CITY—SPECULATION IN CITY LOTS—ENCROACHMENTS ON THE PLAN.

The following extracts from a letter of the President to the Secretary of State will show when, and on what terms, the site was ceded to the Government:

MOUNT VERNON, *March* 31, 1791.

DEAR SIR: Having been so fortunate as to reconcile the contending interests of Georgetown and Carrollsburgh, and to unite them in such an agreement as permits the public purposes to be carried into effect on an extensive and proper scale, I have the pleasure to transmit to you the enclosed proclamation, which, after annexing the seal of the United States, and your counter-signature, you will cause to be published.

The terms entered into by me, on the part of the United States, with the landholders of Georgetown and Carrollsburgh, are, that all the land from Rock Creek, along the river, to the Eastern Branch, and so upwards to or above the ferry, including a breadth of about a mile and a half, the whole containing from three to five thousand acres, is ceded to the public on condition that when the whole shall be surveyed and laid off as a city, (which Major L'Enfant is now directed to do,) the present proprietors shall retain every other lot; and for such part of the land as may be taken for public use, for squares, walks, &c., they shall be allowed at the rate of £25 per acre, the public having the right to reserve such parts of the wood on the land as may be thought necessary to be preserved for ornament. The landholders to have the use and profits of the grounds until the city is laid off into lots, and sale is made of those lots, which, by this agreement, become public property. Nothing is to be allowed for the ground which may be occupied for streets and alleys. * * * *

It was found, on running the lines, that the comprehension of Bladensburgh within them, must have occasioned the exclusion of more important objects; and of this I am convinced, as well by my own observation as Mr. Elliott's opinion.

With regard and esteem, I am, dear sir,
Your most obedient servant,
GEORGE WASHINGTON.

Extract from Mr. Jefferson's reply.

PHILADELPHIA, *April* 10, 1791.

The acquisition of ground at Georgetown is really noble, considering that only £25 an acre is to be paid for any grounds taken for the public, and the streets not to be counted, which will, in fact, reduce it to about £19 an acre. I think very liberal reserves should be made for the public.

A more beautiful site for a city could hardly be obtained. From a point where the Potomac, at a distance of 295 miles from the ocean, and flowing from northwest to southeast, expands to the width of a mile, extended back an almost level plain, hemmed in by a series of gradually sloping hills, terminating with the heights of Georgetown; the plain being nearly three miles in length, from east to west, and varying from a quarter of a mile to one mile in breadth; bounded on the east by the Eastern Branch of the Potomac, where are now the Navy Yard and Congressional cemetery, and on the west by the Rock Creek, which separates it from Georgetown. The small stream from the north, over which the railroad bridge now passes, on entering the city, emptied into a bay or inlet of the Potomac, about 400 feet wide, which jutted in from the west to within a quarter of a mile of the Capitol Hill, and nearly divided the plan. Not far from the head of this, and south of the Capitol Hill, a small stream took its rise in a large number of springs, and emptied into the river, at a place now called Greenleaf's Point, formed by the intersection of the Eastern Branch with the Potomac, and was known as James' Creek. There is a stream above Georgetown which has always been called Goose Creek, but, from a certificate of a survey now preserved in the Mayor's office at Washington, dated 1663,* it appears that the inlet from the Potomac

---

* The following is an authentic copy of the original manuscript in the Mayor's office, being the survey thus referred to:

JUNE 5th, 1663.—Laid out for Francis Pope, of this Province, gentleman, a

was then known by the name of *Tiber*, and probably the stream from the north emptying into it bore the same name; so that Moore did injustice to the history of the place, and confounded streams, when he wrote the well-known line—

"And what was Goose Creek once, is Tiber now."

By the same survey it appears that the land, comprising the Capitol Hill, was called *Rome or Room*, two names which seem to have foreshadowed the destiny of the place. Mr. Force, of Washington, suggests that they probably originated in the fact that the name of the owner of the estate was *Pope*, and, in selecting a name for his plantation, he fancied the title of "Pope of Rome."

In his observations on the river Potomac, published in 1793, Mr. Andrew Ellicott, who afterwards assisted in laying out the city, remarks as follows: "No place has greater advantages of water, either for the supply of the city, or for cleaning the streets, than this ground. The most obvious source is from the head waters of Rock Creek, which takes its rise in ground higher than the city, and can readily be conveyed to every part of it. But the grand object for this purpose, which has been contemplated by those best acquainted with the country hereabouts, and the circumstances attending it, and which has been examined with an eye to this purpose, by good judges, is the Potomac. The water of the river, above the Great Falls, fourteen miles from the city, is 108 feet higher than the tide-water. A small branch, called 'Watts' Branch,' just above the falls, goes in a direction towards the city. From this branch to the city, a canal may be made, (and the ground

---

parcel of land in Charles county, called Room, lying on the east side of the Anacostia river, beginning with a marked oak standing by the river side, the bounded tree of Capt. Robert Troop, and running north by the river for breadth and length 200 ps., to a bounded oak standing at the mouth of a bay or inlet called Tiber; bounding on the north by the said belt, and line drawn east for the length of 320 ps., to a bounded tree standing in the woods; on the east, with a line drawn south from the end of the former line, until you meet with the exterior bounded tree of Robt. Troop, called Scotland Yard; on the south, with the said land; on the west, with the said river, containing, and now laid out for, 400 acres, more or less.

June 5th, 1663.—Laid out for Capt. Robt. Troop, of this Province, a parcel of land in Charles county called Scotland Yard, lying on the east side of the Anacostia river, beginning at a bounded hickory standing by the river side, and running north by the river for breadth the length of 250 ps., to a bounded oak; bounding on the north with a line drawn east into the woods for the length of 320 ps., to a bounded oak; on the east, with a line drawn south from the end of the former line, until you intersect a parallel line drawn from the first bounded hickory; on the south, with the said parallel; on the west, with said river, containing, and now laid out for, 500 acres, more or less.

Below is written: Valuable and ancient documents in relation to the taking up of the tract of land called *Rome*, on the site of which now stands the city of Washington, respectfully presented to the Mayor and Councils of the city by

April 26, 1837. ROB. Y. BRENT.

admits of it very well,) into which the river, or any part of it, may be turned and carried through the city. By this means the water may not only be carried over the highest ground in the city, but, if necessary, over the tops of the houses." The advantages which would thus be presented for mill-seats, are also dwelt upon by Mr. Ellicott, and the whole plan subsequently attracted much attention, having been proposed to Congress by President Jefferson.*

It is said that Washington's attention had been called to the advantages which this place presents for a city, as long previous as when he had been a youthful surveyor of the country round, and that he encamped with Braddock's forces on the hill now occupied by the Observatory, which was long known as Camp Hill, from this circumstance. His judgment was confirmed by the fact that two towns were afterwards planned on the spot, and the first maps of the city represent it as laid out over the plans of Hamburgh and Carrollsville.

Commissioners had been appointed to carry out the objects of the act, and, on the 15th day of April, 1791, the Hon. Daniel Carroll and Dr. David Stuart, superintended the fixing of the first corner-stone of the District of Columbia, at Jones' Point, near Alexandria, where it was laid with all the Masonic ceremonies usual at that time. The following address, delivered by the Rev. James Muir, on that occasion, is copied from a number of the United States Gazette, for 1791:

"Of America, it may be said, as of Judea of old, that it is a good land and large—a land of brooks of waters, of fountains and depths that spring out of the valleys and hills—a land of wheat and barley, and vines, and fig-trees and pomegranates—a land of oil, olives, and honey—a land wherein we eat bread without scarceness, and have lack of nothing—a land whose stones are iron, and out of whose hills thou mayest dig brass—a land which the Lord thy God careth for—the eyes of the Lord thy God are always upon it, from the beginning of the year, even unto the end of the year. May Americans be grateful and virtuous, and they shall insure the indulgence of Providence. May they be unanimous and just, and they shall rise to greatness. May true patriotism actuate every heart. May it be the devout and universal wish, Peace be within thy wall, O America, and prosperity within thy palaces! Amiable it is for brethren to dwell together in unity; it is more fragrant than the perfumes

* A survey with a view to the introduction of water, was made by order of Congress and the city authorities, in 1851, by Lieut. Col. Hughes, of the Topographical Engineers, and he concurs in the opinions expressed by Ellicott. A more careful and complete survey was made in 1853, by Lieut. Meigs, with the same conclusions, and the particular result of his investigations is given further on. The following are given by Col. Hughes as the levels of some of the more prominent points within the city, above ordinary low tide:

Foundation of St. John's Church	65.50
Corner of I and 13th streets west	82.10
Base of Observatory	96.20
Eastern base of Capitol	89.50
Corner of N and 11th streets west	103.70

on Aaron's garment: it is more refreshing than the dews on Hermon's Hill! May this stone long commemorate the goodness of God in those uncommon events which have given America a name among nations. Under this stone may jealousy and selfishness be forever buried. From this stone may a superstructure arise, whose glory, whose magnificence, whose stability, unequalled hitherto, shall astonish the world, and invite even the savage of the wilderness to take shelter under its roof."*

The proceedings in reference to the opening of a national city, appear to have awakened much interest in all parts of the country. In an extra number of the Herald, published at Philadelphia, on the 4th January, 1795, we find a long article, setting forth the general plan, and, more particularly, the designs for improving the mall. It commences thus:

"To found a city, in the centre of the United States, for the purpose of making it the depository of the acts of the Union, and the sanctuary of the laws, which must, one day, rule all North America, is a grand and comprehensive idea, which has already become, with propriety, the object of public respect. In reflecting on the importance of the Union, and on the advantages which it secures to all the inhabitants of the United States, collectively, or to individuals, where is there an American who does not see, in the establishment of a Federal town, a natural means for confirming forever that valuable connection, to which the nation is indebted for liberation from the British yoke? The Federal city, situated in the centre of the United States, is a temple erected to liberty; and towards this edifice will the wishes and expectations of all true friends of their country be incessantly directed. The city of Washington, considered under such important points of view, could not be calculated on a small scale; its extent, the disposition of its avenues and public squares, should all correspond with the magnitude of the object for which it was intended—and we need only cast our eyes upon the situation and plan of the city, to recognize in them the comprehensive genius of the President, to whom the direction of the business has been committed by Congress."

The first public communication on record, in relation to arrangements for laying out this city, is from the pen of General Washington, dated on the 11th March, 1791. In a subsequent letter of the 30th April, 1791, he calls it the Federal city. The name which it now bears, was adopted about four months afterwards, probably without the knowledge of Washington, in a letter to Major L'Enfant, by the first Commissioners, Messrs. Johnson, Stuart, and Carroll, which bears date Georgetown, September 9th, 1791, and informs the architect that they have agreed that the Federal district shall be called "The Territory of Columbia," and the Federal City, "The City of Washington," and directs him to entitle his map accordingly.†

* By the retrocession of Alexandria, this stone is no longer within the limits of the District. A square mass of masonry near the National Monument was the centre of the District.

† Historical Sketches of the Ten-miles Square, by Jonathan Elliot.

On the 18th September, 1793, the southeast corner stone of the north wing of the Capitol was laid by General Washington; the following account of the ceremony, copied from a Georgetown paper into the Maryland Gazette, published at Annapolis, September 26, 1793, has been furnished by D. Claude, jr. Esq. of that city. The orator of the day, was Joseph Claude, architect of the State House of Annapolis:

GEORGETOWN, *September* 21, 1793.

On Wednesday one of the grandest Masonic processions took place for the purpose of laying the corner stone of the Capitol of the United States, which perhaps ever was exhibited on the like important occasion. About 10 o'clock Lodge No. 9 was visited by that congregation so graceful to the craft, Lodge No. 22 of Virginia, with all their officers and regalia; and directly afterwards appeared, on the southern banks of the grand river Potomac, one of the finest companies of volunteer artillery that hath been lately seen, parading to receive the President of the United States, who shortly came in sight with his suite, to whom the artillery paid their military honors; and his Excellency and suite crossed the Potomac, and was received in Maryland by the officers and Brethren of No. 22 Virginia, and No. 9 Maryland, whom the President headed, and preceded by a band of music; the rear brought up by the Alexandria volunteer artillery, with grand solemnity of march, proceeded to the President's square, in the City of Washington, where they were met and saluted by No. 15 of the City of Washington, in all their elegant badges and clothing, headed by brother Joseph Clark, Rt. W. G. M., P. T., and conducted to a large lodge prepared for the purpose of their reception. After a short space of time, by the vigilance of Brother Clotworthy Stephenson, Grand Marshal P. T., the brotherhood and other bodies were disposed in a second order of procession, which took place amidst a brilliant crowd of spectators of both sexes, according to the following arrangement, viz:

The Surveying Department of the city of Washington.
Mayor and Corporation of Georgetown.
Virginia Artillery.
Commissioners of the city of Washington and their attendants.
Stone-cutters. Mechanics.

[Here follow all the various officers of Free Masonry, amongst whom appears Grand Master P. T. George Washington, Worshipful Master of No. 22, Virginia.]

The procession marched two abreast, in the greatest solemn dignity, with music playing, drums beating, colors flying, and spectators rejoicing, from the President's square to the Capitol, in the city of Washington, where the Grand Marshal ordered a halt, and directed each file in the procession to incline two steps, one to the right and one to the left, and faced each other, which formed a hollow oblong square, through which the Grand Sword Bearer led the van, followed by the Grand Master P. T. on the left, the President of the United States in the centre, and the Worshipful Master of No. 22 Virginia on the right; all the other orders that composed the procession advanced in the reverse of their order of march from the President's square to the southeast corner of the Capitol, and the artillery filed off to a destined ground to display their manœuvres and discharge their cannon; the President of the United States, the Grand Master P. T., and Worshipful Master of No. 22 taking their stand to the east of a huge stone, and all the craft forming a circle westward, stood a short time in awful order.

The Artillery discharged a volley.

The Grand Marshal delivered the Commissioners a large silver plate with an inscription thereon, which the Commissioners ordered to be read, and was as follows:

"This southeast corner stone of the Capitol of the United States of America, in the city of Washington, was laid on the 18th day of September, 1793, in in the thirteenth year of American Independence, in the first year of the second term of the Presidency of George Washington, whose virtues in the civil administration of his country have been so conspicuous and beneficial, as his military valor and prudence have been useful in establishing her liberties, and in the year of Masonry, 5793, by the President of the United States, in concert with the Grand Lodge of Maryland, several lodges under its jurisdiction, and Lodge No. 22 from Alexandria, Virginia.

"Thomas Johnson, David Stuart, and Daniel Carroll, Commissioners; Joseph Clarke, R. W. G. M. P. T.; James Hoban and Stephen Hallate, Architects; Collin Williamson, M. Mason."

The artillery discharged a volley.

The plate was then delivered to the President, who, attended by the Grand Master P. T. and three most Worshipful Masters, descended to the cavazion trench and deposed the plate, and laid it on the corner-stone of the Capitol of the United States of America, on which was deposed corn, wine, and oil, when the whole congregation joined in reverential prayer, which was succeeded by Masonic chanting honors, and a volley from the artillery.

The President of the United States and his attendant brethren ascended from the cavazion to the east of the corner-stone, and there the Grand Master P. T., elevated on a triple rostrum, delivered an oration fitting the occasion, which was received with brotherly love and commendation. At intervals, during the delivery of the oration, several volleys were discharged by the artillery. The ceremony ended in prayer, Masonic chanting honors, and a 15-volley from the artillery.

The whole company retired to an extensive booth, where an ox of 500 lbs. weight was barbecued, of which the company generally partook, with every abundance of other recreation. The festival concluded with fifteen successive volleys from the artillery, whose military discipline and manœuvres merit every commendation.

Before dark the whole company departed with joyful hopes of the production of their labor.

It is related that the President, when offered by a physician present the use of the only umbrella which the company possessed, to shield him from the rays of the sun, declined it with the remark, "To the ladies with it doctor, I have been exposed to the sun *before* in the course of my life;" which, from the manner of its utterance, made a great impression on the hearers, as one of the few instances in which Washington joked or smiled.

The following extract from the letter of Mr. Jefferson, already referred to, will show the interest which that distinguished statesman took in the plans:

"I received, last night, from Major L'Enfant, a request to furnish him any plans of towns I could for his examination; I accordingly send him, by this post, plans of Frankfort-on-the-Mayne, Carlsruhe, Amsterdam, Strasburgh, Paris, Orleans, Bordeaux, Lyons, Montpelier, Marseilles, Turin, and Milan, on large and accurate scales, which I preserved while in those towns respectively. They are none of them comparable to the Old Babylon, revived in Philadelphia, and exemplified. While in Europe, I selected about a dozen or two of the handsomest fronts of private buildings, of which I have the plates. Perhaps it might decide the taste of the new town, were these to be engraved and distributed, gratis, among the inhabitants of Georgetown. The expense would be trifling."

In Washington's correspondence, we find frequent allusions to discussions had with the architect here referred to—Major L'Enfant, a Frenchman of talent, but apparently obstinate and unwilling to be advised by others. His plan, though attractive in the outline upon paper, was, in many respects, an exceedingly impracticable one, and led to the sacrifice of one or two of the most beautiful eminences in the city.

He first laid down two sets of streets, distinguished by letters and numbers, concerning which the French minister jocosely remarked, "that L'Enfant was not only a child in name, but in education also; as from the name he gave the streets, he appeared to know little else than A B C, and 1 2 3." It appears, however, by a letter of the Commissioners, that they gave these names to the streets at the same time with that to the city; and it was, we think, a good arrangement, since the streets could more easily be found by a stranger under such designations.

The names of some of the Avenues were also probably given by them. Others have been named since, such as Louisiana, Indiana, and Ohio.*

The lettered and numbered streets intersect each other at right-angles, as at Philadelphia; and had he stopped here, he would have consulted the interests of those who were to have erected private buildings; but there would have been nothing in it sufficiently distinctive of the national character of the city. It was desirable to bring the public buildings into view from the most distant quarters, that there

* The names of the thirteen States were engraved upon a bridge over Rock creek, constructed of refuse materials taken from the public buildings, since carried away. That of Pennsylvania was on the key-stone; hence the name "Key-stone State."

might be direct communication with them all. Accordingly, immense avenues, varying from a hundred to a hundred and sixty feet in width, were made to radiate from particular points, such as the Capitol and the President's house; the consequence is, that, in the first place, there are twice as many streets as are required; and, in the second place, the avenues, intersecting the rectangular streets, cut up the squares into triangles and oblongs, spoil the most prominent corner lots, and leave every where awkward spaces.*

The design of these avenues was a grand feature, worthy of the nation; but the architect should either have laid them down first, to serve, as it were, for the great arteries of the city, and then, taking these as base lines, made such other streets to connect as necessity required; or he should, in the first instance, have marked out a much smaller number of rectangular streets. Thus, the building-lots on the side streets would have been sufficiently large to admit of court-yards in front, with appropriate shubbery, and made it in a short time, with a small population, a really attractive "*rus in urbe*," after the style of New Haven, Hartford, and the more retired parts of Richmond. To make matters worse, a regulation was made prohibiting the enclosure of more than five feet of the street in a court-yard.

The eminence over which Louisiana avenue is made to climb, and which will be more generally recognized as the site of the City Hall, should have been entirely reserved for some public purpose, instead of

---

* In the map first submitted to Congress, are the following remarks:

"The grand avenues, and such streets as lead immediately to public places, are from 130 to 160 feet wide, and may be conveniently divided into foot-ways, walks of trees, and a carriage way. The other streets are from 90 to 110 feet wide."

In order to execute this plan, Mr. Ellicott drew a true meridional line by celestial observation, which passes through the area intended for the Capitol. These lines were accurately measured and made the basis upon which the whole plan was executed. He ran all the lines by a transit instrument, and determined the acute angles by actual measurement, and left nothing to the uncertainty of the compass.

The positions for the different edifices, and for the several squares or areas of different shapes as they were laid down, were first determined on the most advantageous ground, commanding the most extensive prospects, and the better susceptible of such improvements as either use or ornament may hereafter call for.

Lines or avenues of direct communication have been devised to connect the separate and most distant objects with the principal, and to preserve through the whole a reciprocity of sight at the same time. Attention has been paid to the passing of those leading avenues over the most favorable ground for prospect and convenience.

North and south lines, intersected by others running due east and west, have made the distribution of the city into streets, squares, &c.; and those lines have been so combined as to meet at certain given points with those divergent avenues, so as to form on the spaces "first determined" the different squares or areas.

being traversed by three or four streets, so near each other as to make it impossible to erect other than small slender two-story houses.

We speak thus particularly, relative to the defects in the plan, in order to show the changes which have been made in the appearance of the ground, and to shift the censure for any want of beauty that may present itself in the present aspect of the site, from those who made the selection, to those who abused its advantages by adopting such a design. But, on the other hand, there is much that is beautiful in the plan; and, if Congress were but reasonably liberal in their ideas, we might hope to see it developed to a much greater extent in the course of one or two years.

In the original plan of the city, as submitted to Congress by the President, in January, 1790, mention is made of the subjoined magnificent intentions:

1. "An equestrian figure of George Washington, a monument voted in 1783, by the late Continental Congress."

It was not until 1852 that Congress made an appropriation for this statue; but, in the meantime, the site thus designated for it, in Washington's lifetime, has been given by Congress for the Washington National Monument, now in progress of construction.

2. "An historic column, also intended for a mile or itinerary column, from whose station (at a mile from the Federal House) all distances and places through the continent are to be calculated."

The site designated for this was at the open space east of the Capitol, at the intersection of East Capitol street, North Carolina, Massachusetts, Kentucky, and Tennessee avenues.

3. "A naval itinerary column, proposed to be erected to celebrate the first rise of a navy, and to stand a ready monument to perpetuate its progress and achievements.

4. "Fifteen squares were to be divided among the several States in the Union for each of them to improve; the centres of these squares designed for statues columns, obelisks, &c., such as the different States may choose to erect.

5. "A church intended for national purposes, such public prayer, thanksgivings, funeral orations, &c., and assigned to the special use of no particular sect or denomination, but equally open to all. It will likewise be a proper shelter for such monuments as were voted by the late Continental Congress, for those heroes who fell in the cause of liberty, and for such others as may hereafter be decreed by the voice of a grateful nation."

The square now occupied by the Patent Office was intended for this church, which was to be officiated in by the chaplains of Congress.

6. "Five grand fountains, intended with a constant spout of water."

These were to be at reservation 17—intersection of F street north and Maryland avenue, H street north and New York avenue, H street north and Pennsylvania avenue, and Market space.

7. "A grand avenue, four hundred feet in breadth, and about a mile in length, bordered with gardens, ending in a slope from the houses on each side. This avenue leads to the monument of Washington, and connects the Congress garden with the President's park."

This is the ground* extending from the Capitol to the monument on the Potomac, and known as the mall. Nothing was ever done towards improving it, until 1851–'2, when, Congress having made an appropriation towards that object, President Fillmore engaged the services of the late A. J. Downing, landscape gardener, who laid out the grounds upon a plan which was a great improvement upon the original design. It consists of serpentine walks and drives, with arrangements for presenting all the forest trees of the country, as well as the accommodation of a botanic garden, should Congress authorize one. That portion in front of the Smithsonian Institute, and immediately south of the President's house, has been planted; the rest is unfinished, and no part has as yet been suitably enclosed.

---

* To give some idea of the extent of this ground, we annex the following statement from the Surveyor's office—also, the size of Judiciary, or City Hall Square:

1st. The distance from the north side of the canal to the north side of south B street, is	1602.41 feet.
The canal along the north side of the wall is 146 feet wide, and the street which intervenes between the mall and the canal, is 80 feet wide. Deducting, then, from the distance given above, 146+80=	226.00 "
We have, for the width of the mall	1376.41 "
2d. The area of the mall, between Seventh and Twelfth streets, (being 1669.41 feet on east and west, and 1376.41 feet north and south line,) is	52.75 acres.
The portion between Twelfth and Fourteenth streets, (being 973.58×1376.41 feet,) contains	30.76 "
And the portion between Fourteenth and Fifteenth streets, (being 483.54×1376.41 feet,) contains	15.29 "
Making the total area of the mall, *from* Seventh *to* Fifteenth street, exclusive of the space occupied by Twelfth and Fourteenth streets	98.80 "
3d. The portion of the mall granted to the Smithsonian Institution, (that is, the portion included between Ninth and Twelfth streets and south B, and the prolongation of the centre line of East Capitol being 1087.08×759.75 feet,) contains	18.96 "
4th. That portion of Judiciary Square which is south of the south side of E street, contains 236,838 square feet, equal to	5.46 "

5th. The distance from Pennsylvania Avenue, on the streets, at present bridged, to the south side of the mall, is as follows:

On Fourteenth street	2,965 feet.
On Twelfth street	2,581 "
On Seventh street	1,932 "

8. "The water of Tiber Creek to be conveyed to the high ground, where the Congress House stands, and, after watering that part of the city, its overplus will fall from under the base of the edifice, and, in a cascade of twenty feet in height, and fifty in breadth, into the reservoir below, thence to run, in three falls, through the gardens in the grand canal."

Instead of this last, a spring of water was some years since conducted to the Capitol, affording but an insufficient supply for that edifice and Pennsylvania avenue. Should the water-works now in progress be completed, an opportunity will be afforded of carrying this plan into execution, and thus keep the canal constantly full, and make it rather ornamental than otherwise, (especially if it be made serpentine, as proposed by Downing,) while still answering its present purpose of drainage, and communication from the Chesapeake and Ohio Canal to the Navy Yard.

The feature of connecting the Capitol and President's House by a garden, is calculated to soften the distance between these two edifices somewhat, as in the case of the Chamber of Deputies and Tuilleries at Paris, which, no doubt, L'Enfant had in his eye when he made the plan. Until this is carried out, the two sections of the city on different sides of the canal will never look well, for want of any appropriate connection; and, not only this, but the Capitol grounds, (which by this garden would, to all intents, extend to the Potomac,) must present a half finished appearance.

From the figures drawn on some of the early maps, and one or two other circumstances, we are led to infer that it was also, at one time, proposed that one side of this mall should be, in part, lined with public buildings or residences for the heads of departments and foreign ministers. It is well known that a portion of the President's square was, at one time, set apart for the Portuguese minister. In a report of the Commissioners to Congress, made March 23d, 1802, we find the following statement:

"The measure of granting sites for the residences of foreign ministers was warmly recommended by President Washington, and approved by President Adams, before any steps were taken by the Commissioners to carry it into effect. President Washington, himself, pointed out the spot granted to the Queen of Portugal, as a proper site for the residence of a foreign minister, and Mr. Adams delivered letters from the Commissioners, making the offer to all the ministers of friendly powers near the United States, and endorsed his approbation of the deed to the Queen of Portugal, after it was executed. But the Attorney-General was of opinion that Congress, alone, were competent to make the grant—an idea which never occurred to either of the President's, or any of the Commissioners."

Some years since, Congress very unwisely reduced the size of these public grounds by selling out, for private purposes, portions of them near the Capitol, marked on the map as squares A, B, C, and D, and reservations 10 and 12. The effect of this is to reduce the mall to an awkward point at Third street, and materially embarrass the plans for improvement.

The "magnificent distances" at which the executive are separated from the legislative departments, have been made a ground of complaint; but we think there was much judgment shown in the choice of these situations. A suitable and prominent position was assigned to each edifice, which could not have been the case had they all been congregated in one place, unless a structure as large as the palace of Versailles had been erected, (and this would not only have been cumbrous and inconvenient in many respects, but unsafe; as, in case of fire or invasion, the whole building would become a sacrifice to the flames, or the explosive compound.) Again, it was thought that their immediate vicinity to the legislative halls would offer a great temptation to the clerks to neglect their duties, in order to hear the debates, and that the constant intrusion of members of Congress would interrupt the public business. General Washington, in a letter written shortly before his death, thus speaks of a suggestion made by Mr. Adams, to place the departments near the Capitol: "The principles which operated for fixing the site for the two principal buildings, were understood and found necessary, at the time, to obtain the primary object—i. e., the ground and means for either purpose; but it is always easy, from an ignorant or partial view of a measure, to distort and place it in an unfavorable attitude. Where or how the houses for the President, and the public offices may be fixed, is to me, as an individual, a matter of moonshine. But, the reverse of the President's motive for placing the latter near the Capitol, was my motive for fixing them by the former. The daily intercourse which the secretaries of the departments must have with the President, would render a distant situation extremely inconvenient to them, and not much less so would one be close to the Capitol; for it was the universal complaint of them all, that, while the legislature was in session, they could do little or no business, so much were they interrupted by the individual visits of members, (in office hours,) and by calls for papers. Many of them have disclosed to me that they have been obliged often to go home and deny themselves, in order to transact the current business."

Nor could any reasonable estimate be made as to the probable wants of government, in the way of public erections. All the archives of the Treasury, War, State, Indian, and Pension Departments, were formerly kept in two buildings—now, the Treasury, alone, occupies an edifice as large as six of those; it was important, then, that each department should have a building to itself so constructed that it might, at any future time, be enlarged without marring its appearance, and in the immediate neighborhood for the residences of the officers employed therein. But it was probably not intended that the executive officers should be scattered as they are. The Patent Office square was, as we have seen, reserved for a church. The General Post Office Department owes its present position to the circumstance that a brick building, erected for a hotel, was rented by the Government for the temporary accommodation of Congress, after the burning of the Capitol, and then purchased for the Post Office and Patent Office, in the absence of other accommodations. And a gross encroachment on the plan has been committed in the location, by President Jackson, of the Treasury building. That structure, when finished, will be a noble edifice, and will have probably cost $1,200,000; but it is so badly situated as to ruin its appearance, and entirely exclude from view the President's house, and to obstruct the distant and beautiful prospect from the East room of that edifice, through the line of F street. The building, although nearly four hundred feet in length, will scarcely be visible except from the street immediately before it; and the three finest porticoes will front upon the President's kitchen garden. The necessity is involved of taking down the State Department, which has cost upwards of $90,000, and, also, of erecting a building to correspond for the other department on the west side of the executive mansion; a blunder entirely inexcusable when there were so many excellent sites at command, and especially when the map of 1792 distinctly designated positions on either side of the President's house, south of Pennsylvania and New York avenues, which would have been equally as accessible, given a far more imposing aspect to the buildings, and preserved a distinct view of the President's house in every direction. Experience has proved the truth of the positions taken by Washington, in a letter to the Commissioners, dated December 26, 1796, where he remarks: "I have never yet met with a single instance where it has been proposed to depart from the published plan of the city, that an inconvenience or dispute of some sort has not sooner or later occurred; for which reason I am persuaded that there should be no departure from it, but in cases of necessity or very obvious utility."

When the plans of the new city were completed, they were sent to all parts of the country and to Europe, (an act having been passed to enable aliens to hold land there,) and the bidding was very high for the best lots. Any one who stands on the dome of the Capitol, will observe the wide space which intervenes between the navy-yard and Greenleaf's Point, (where are the arsenal and penitentiary.) It was supposed by many that this part would be built up first, and immense sums were here thrown away in city lots; the course which things took afterwards, having ruined the proprietors. The change was chiefly brought about by the circumstance that, when Congress was first established there, the members boarded in Georgetown, for the want of sufficient accommodations elsewhere; and, also, to the fact that the public offices were in that direction, which caused the Pennsylvania avenue to be first improved.

Some idea of the magnitude of the plans may be formed from the following statement of its present size:

"The city extends, from northwest to southeast, about four miles and a half; and, from east to southwest, about two miles and a half. Its circumference is fourteen miles, and aggregate length of the streets is one hundred and ninety-nine miles, and of the avenues sixty-five miles. The avenues, streets, and open spaces, contain three thousand six hundred and four acres; and the public reservations, exclusive of reservations ten, eleven, and twelve, since disposed of for private purposes, five hundred and thirteen acres. The whole area of the squares of the city amounts to one hundred and thirty-one million six hundred and eighty-four thousand one hundred and seventy-six square feet, or three thousand and sixteen acres; one-half of which, fifteen hundred and eight acres, was reserved for the use of the United States, and the remaining half assigned to the original proprietors; fifteen hundred and thirty-six acres belonged to the United States."*

If we have made ourselves understood in our remarks, it must appear that, although perhaps more extensive than was necessary, the whole plan is not to be condemned because not already occupied with a population proportionate to its pretensions. It must be remembered that it is laid out for a future as well as a present generation. Would that the old Knickerbockers had looked forward as much, and made half the provisions for wide streets and ventilation, which has been done at the city of Washington! Every possible want of the Government, for centuries to come, is here anticipated. But it will be shown hereafter that, as it is a plan suited only for a Government city, the Government must contribute its share towards filling it up.

---

* Watterston's New Guide to Washington.

CHAPTER III.

EMBARRASSMENTS AND REMEDIES—WASHINGTON'S LETTER TO THE GOVERNOR OF MARYLAND, ASKING FOR A LOAN—ACKNOWLEDGING LOAN—RELATIVE TO WORK ON PUBLIC BUILDINGS—HIS DEATH—OCCUPATION OF CITY BY GOVERNMENT AND CONGRESS, AND ADDRESSES ON THE OCCASION—APPEARANCE OF THE CITY AT THIS TIME DESCRIBED IN LETTERS OF JOHN COTTON SMITH, OLIVER WOLCOTT, AND MRS. PRESIDENT ADAMS—PROGRESS OF THE CITY, AND CAUSES WHICH RETARDED ITS GROWTH—LOTTERY DEBT—CHESAPEAKE AND OHIO CANAL—WHY SHOULD CONGRESS EXPEND SO MUCH TIME AND MONEY ON THE DISTRICT?—WANT OF SUFFICIENT LEGISLATION—PLANNED RATHER FOR THE COUNTRY AT LARGE, THAN THE CONVENIENCE OF PRESENT INHABITANTS—FUND DERIVED FROM CITY LOTS—EXPENDITURES BY THE CITY ON IMPROVEMENTS—VALUE OF PRIVATE AND PUBLIC PROPERTY—SHOULD THE NATION PAY TAXES?—ABSENCE OF SYSTEM IN EXPENDITURES OF THE GOVERNMENT AND THE CITY—ALL OBLIGATIONS WILL BE REDEEMED BY WATER WORKS—THEIR COST AND IMPORTANCE—REPRESENTATION NOT DESIRED—MR. WEBSTER'S ADDRESS ON LAYING CORNER-STONE OF CAPITOL EXTENSION.

It was not without the most untiring exertions on the part of General Washington, that sufficient means were obtained for the completion of the public buildings by the time specified, (1800.) An immense pile of correspondence carried on by him with both public and private individuals, up to the very close of his life, attests the intense interest which he took in whatever pertained to the establishment and prosperity of the city. Many of these letters relate to the progress of the public buildings, especially the Capitol, to the prompt completion of which he seems to have looked as an event almost ominous of the permanent establishment of the Government at this place. Virginia had made a donation of $120,000,* and Maryland one of $72,000—these were now exhausted. After various efforts to raise money by the forced sales of public lots, and after abortive attempts to borrow money at home and abroad, on the credit of these lots; amidst general embarrassment, whilst Congress withheld any aid whatever, the urgency appeared to the President so great, as to induce him to make a personal application to the State of Maryland for a loan. Nothing can exceed the characteristic force with which it is written, or more strikingly exhibit the imperative necessity which overruled all etiquette and form; for it seems that the Attorney-General had expressed some doubts as to the propriety of such

* Within a few years a claim has been presented to Congress for this amount by the Orange and Alexandria Railroad Company, as assignee of the interest of the State of Virginia, on the ground that it was a loan and not a donation. This claim was very ably reviewed by Senator Broadhead in a report, (Senate doc., 32d Congress, 1st session, No. 49,) in which many points dwelt upon in our first chapter are discussed at length, and the conclusion arrived at, that Virginia and Maryland made these donations to secure the Seat of Government in their midst, with no thought of repayment.

a letter, it not having been usual for the President to correspond, but by the channels of certain officers, who, in this instance, would be the Commissioners.

George Washington to his Excellency, J. H. Stone, Governor of Maryland.

PHILADELPHIA, *Dec.* 7, 1796.

SIR: The attempts lately made by the Commissioners of the city of Washington to borrow money in Europe, for the purpose of carrying on the public buildings, having failed or been retarded, they have been authorized by me to apply to your State for a loan of one hundred and fifty thousand dollars, upon terms which they will communicate. Such is the present condition of foreign nations with respect to money, that, according to the best information, there is no reasonable hope of obtaining a loan in any of them immediately, and application can now only be made in the United States upon this subject with any prospect of success, and perhaps nowhere with greater propriety than to the legislature of Maryland; where, it must be presumed, the most anxious solicitude is felt for the growth and prosperity of that city, which is intended for the permanent Seat of Government for America.

If the State has it in its power to lend the money which is solicited, I persuade myself it will be done; and the more especially at this time, when a loan is so indispensable, that, without it, not only very great and many impediments must be induced in the prosecution of the work now in hand, but inevitable loss must be sustained by the funds of the city, in consequence of premature sales of public property. I have thought I ought not to omit to state, for the information of the General Assembly, as well the difficulty of obtaining money on loan, as the present necessity for it; which I must request the favor of you most respectfully to communicate.

The application was successful, and the State of Maryland, while complying with the personal request of the President for a loan, passed resolutions in testimony of their high regard for Washington himself. The amount loaned was $100,000; and it exhibits the deplorable credit of the General Government, at that time, when a State called upon the private credit of the Commissioners, as an additional guarantee of the repayment of the loan.

Washington to Gustavus Scott, one of the Commissioners, on learning the action of Maryland.

PHILADELPHIA, *December* 26, 1796.

SIR: Your favor of the 15th inst. was not received until the 22d; to what the delay is to be ascribed I know not.

The voice of Maryland, as expressed by its Legislature in the resolutions which you enclosed, is flattering indeed, as respects myself personally, and highly pleasing as relates to their federal sentiments. I thank you for sending them.

From what you have said of the disposition of the Senate of that State, the presumption is, that the loan of $100,000, for the use of the Federal city, must, ere this, have passed through all the requisite forms. The necessity of the case justified the obtaining it almost on any terms; and the zeal of the Commissioners (if they in their individual capacities, which they surely may do, without hazarding anything) in making themselves liable for the amount, as it could not be had without, cannot fail of approbation. At the same time, I must confess that the request has a very singular appearance, and will not, I should suppose, be very grateful to the feelings of Congress.

Washington to the Commissioners of the City of Washington, relative to work on Public Buildings.

February 15*th*, 1797.

GENTLEMEN: Several of your letters have been received within a few days; and notwithstanding the accumulation of business consequent of the near epoch for my quitting the chair of government, the receipt of them should not have remained so long unacknowledged, had I not placed such as related to the power of attorney and to some disputed points into the hands of the Law Officer of the United States, for his official opinion, without having received his report, owing, I believe, to his having been hurried almost as much as myself.

Thus circumstanced, I shall confine the subject of this letter wholly to the expression of my sentiments relative to the public buildings, conceiving it necessary that you should be informed of them without delay.

When, in the course of the Autumn, you suggested the propriety of designating sites for the executive offices, and for providing materials for their erection, I yielded a ready assent; and still think that if we had the means at command, and no doubt was entertained of the adequacy of them, these buildings ought to commence.

But when the difficulty in obtaining loans, and the disadvantageous terms on which money is borrowed has since become so apparent; when I see those whose interest it is to appreciate the credit of the city and to aid the Commissioners in all their laudable exertions, brooding over their jealousies and spreading the seeds of distrust; and when I perceive (as I clearly do) that the public mind is in a state of doubt, if not despair, of having the principal buildings in readiness for Congress by the time contemplated; for these reasons I say, and for others that might be enumerated, I am now decidedly of opinion that the edifices for the executive offices ought to be suspended; that the work on the house for the President should advance no faster (at the expense or retardment of the Capitol) than is necessary to keep pace therewith and to preserve it from injury; and that all the means not essential for other purposes, and all the force, ought to be employed on the Capitol.

It may be relied on that it is the progress of that building that is to inspire or depress public confidence. Under any circumstances, this, more or less, would be the case. But when it is reported by many, and believed by some, (without foundation, I am persuaded,) that there is a bias elsewhere, it is essential, on the score of policy and for the gratification of the public wishes, that the work should be vigorously prosecuted in the manner I have suggested, and I require it accordingly. Considered in a simple point of view, the matter stands thus—are the funds sufficient to accomplish all the objects which are contemplated? If doubts arise, then which of these objects are to be preferred? On this ground, there would be but one opinion; every body would cry out—"the Capitol." Again, admit that the resources will ultimately be adequate, but cannot be drawn forth in the ratio of your general wants, will not the same answer, as it respects time, apply with equal force to the building just mentioned? This, then, appears safe ground to proceed on. It would gratify the public wishes and expectations; might possibly appease clamor; and if all the buildings cannot be completed in time, no material evil would result from the postponement of the subordinate offices until the Capitol is in such a state of forwardness as to remove all doubts of its being ready for the reception of Congress by the time appointed. Another good (mentioned in a former letter) would flow from it; which is, that in proportion as that building advanced and doubts subsided, private buildings would be erected where they are most wanted for the accommodation of the members. The public offices might shift (as they have done) a while longer. I write in much haste for this morning's post, that the letter may get to you in the course of the week. If I have expressed myself in such a manner as to be clearly understood, it is enough.

General Washington did not, however, live to see his wishes fulfilled. He died on the 14th of December, 1799.

The Commissioners reported that the public buildings would be ready for the reception of the Government in the summer of 1800. Accordingly, the executive offices were, in the month of June in that year, removed thither from Philadelphia, and Congress commenced its session there on the third Monday of November following. On this occasion, in his opening speech, President Adams said: "I congratulate the people of the United States on the assembling of Congress at the permanent Seat of their Government; and I congratulate you, gentlemen, on the prospect of a residence not to be exchanged. It would be unbecoming the representatives of this nation to assemble for the first time in this solemn temple, without looking up to the Supreme Ruler of the universe, and imploring his blessing. It is with you, gentlemen, to consider whether the local powers over the District of Columbia, vested by the Constitution in the Congress of the United States, shall be immediately exercised. If, in your opinion, this important trust ought now to be executed, you cannot fail, while performing it, to take into view the future probable situation of the territory, for the happiness of which you are about to provide. You will consider it as the capital of a great nation, advancing with unexampled rapidity in arts, in commerce, in wealth, and in population, and possessing within itself those resources, which, if not thrown away, or lamentably misdirected, will secure to it a long course of prosperity and self-government."

The Senate, in their reply, said: "We meet you, sir, and the other branch of the national legislature, in the city which is honored by the name of our late hero and sage, the illustrious Washington, with sensations and emotions which exceed our power of description."

The House of Representatives, in reply, said: "The final establishment of the Seat of National Government, which has now taken place in the District of Columbia, is an event of no small importance in the political transactions of our country. Nor can we on this occasion omit to express a hope that the spirit which animated the great founder of this city, may descend to future generations; and that the wisdom, magnanimity, and steadiness, which marked the events of his public life, may be imitated in all succeeding ages. A consideration of those powers which have been vested in Congress over the District of Columbia, will not escape our attention; nor shall we forget that, in exercising those powers, a regard must be had to those events which will necessarily attend the capital of America."

We have thus traced the history of our national capital up to the period of its first occupation.

For ten years anterior to the removal of the public offices, it is known traditionally that the area of Washington scarcely contained five hundred inhabitants, most of the houses being mere cabins, erected for the temporary accommodation of laborers.

The appearance of the city at this time is thus described by the Hon. John Cotton Smith, of Connecticut. He was a distinguished member of Congress of the Federal school of politics:

"Our approach to the city was accompanied with sensations not easily described. One wing of the Capitol only had been erected, which, with the President's house, a mile distant from it, both constructed with white sandstone, were shining objects in dismal contrast with the scene around them. Instead of recognising the avenues and streets portrayed on the plan of the city, not one was visible, unless we except a road, with two buildings on each side of it, called the New Jersey avenue. The Pennsylvania, leading, as laid down on paper, from the Capitol to the Presidential mansion, was then nearly the whole distance a deep morass, covered with alder bushes, which were cut through the width of the intended avenue during the then ensuing winter. Between the President's house and Georgetown a block of houses had been erected, which then bore, and may still bear, the name of the *six buildings*. There were also two other blocks, consisting of two or three dwelling houses, in different directions, and now and then an insulated wooden habitation; the intervening spaces, and, indeed, the surface of the city generally, being covered with *shrub oak bushes* on the higher grounds, and on the marshy soil either trees or some sort of shrubbery. Nor was the desolate aspect of the place a little augmented by a number of unfinished edifices at *Greenleaf's Point*, and on an eminence a short distance from it, commenced by an individual whose name they bore, but the state of whose funds compelled him to abandon them, not only unfinished, but in a ruinous condition. There appeared to be but two really comfortable habitations in all respects within the bounds of the city, one of which belonged to Dudley Carroll, Esq., and the other to Notley Young,* who were the former

* This was taken down in 1854, to make room for south G street. It was a fine old structure overlooking the Potomac.

proprietors of a large proportion of the land appropriated to the city, but who reserved for their own accommodation ground sufficient for gardens and other useful appurtenances. The roads in every direction were muddy and unimproved. A sidewalk was attempted in one instance by a covering formed of the chips of the stones which had been hewed for the Capitol. It extended but a little way, and was of little value; for in dry weather the sharp fragments cut our shoes and in wet weather covered them with white mortar. In short, it was a 'new settlement.' The houses, with two or three exceptions, had been very recently erected, and the operation greatly hurried in view of the approaching transfer of the National Government. A laudable desire was manifested by what few citizens and residents there were to render our condition as pleasant as circumstances would permit. One of the blocks of buildings already mentioned was situated on the east side of what was intended for the Capitol square, and, being chiefly occupied by an extensive and well-kept hotel, accommodated a goodly number of the members. Our little party took lodgings with a Mr. Peacock, in one of the houses on the New Jersey avenue, with the addition of Senators Tracy, of Connecticut, and Chipman and Paine, of Vermont; and Representatives Thomas, of Maryland, and Dana, Edmond, and Griswold, of Connecticut. Speaker Sedgwick was allowed a room to himself; the rest of us in pairs. To my excellent friend Davenport and myself was allotted a spacious and decently furnished apartment, with separate beds, on the lower floor. Our diet was various, but always substantial, and we were attended by active and faithful servants. A large proportion of the Southern members took lodgings at Georgetown, which, though of a superior order, were three miles distant from the Capitol, and of course rendered the daily employment of hackney coaches indispensable.

"Notwithstanding the unfavorable aspect which Washington presented on our arrival, I cannot sufficiently express my admiration of its local position. From the Capitol you have a distinct view of its fine undulating surface, situated at the confluence of the Potomac and its eastern branch, the wide expanse of that majestic river to the bend at Mount Vernon, the cities of Alexandria and Georgetown, and the cultivated fields and blue hills of Maryland and Virginia on either side of the river, the whole constituting a prospect of surpassing beauty and grandeur. The city has also the inestimable advantage of delightful water, in many instances flowing from copious springs, and always attainable by digging to a moderate depth; to which may be added the singular fact that such is the due admixture of loam and clay in the soil of a great portion of the city that a house may be built of brick made of the earth dug from the cellar; hence it was not unusual to see the remains of a brick-kiln near the newly erected dwelling house or other edifice. In short, when we consider not only these advantages, but what, in a national point of view, is of superior importance, the location on a fine navigable river, accessible to the whole maratime frontier of the United States, and yet easily rendered defensible against foreign invasion; and that, by the facilities of internal navigation and railways, it may be approached by the population of the Western States, and indeed of the whole nation, with less inconvenience than any other conceivable situation, we must acknowledge that its selection by Washington as the permanent Seat of the Federal Government, affords a striking exhibition of the discernment, wisdom, and forecast, which characterized that illustrious man. Under this impression, whenever, during the six years of my connexion with Congress, the question of removing the Seat of Government to some other place was agitated—and the proposition was frequently made—I stood almost alone as a Northern man in giving my vote in the negative."

In June of 1800, Mr. Oliver Wolcott, then Secretary of the Treasury, taking time by the forelock, came to "the city," that he might ascertain whether the building which had been erected for the accommodation of his department would suffice for that purpose. On the 4th of July he addressed a letter to Mrs. Wolcott, in which he thus describes his first impressions of the city:

"I write this letter in the building erected for the use of the Treasury Department in the city of Washington; and, this being a day of leisure, I shall be able to give you some idea of this famous place, the permanent seat of American Government.

"The city of Washington, *or at least some part of it*, is about forty miles from Baltimore. The situation is pleasant, and indeed beautiful; the prospects are equal to those which are called *good* on Connecticut river; the soil is here called good, but I call it bad. It is an exceedingly stiff reddish clay, which becomes dust in dry, and mortar in rainy weather. * * *

"It [the President's House] was built to be looked at by visiters and strangers, and will render its occupant an object of ridicule with some and of pity with others. It must be cold and damp in winter, and cannot be kept in tolerable order without a regiment of servants.

"The Capitol is situated on an eminence, which I should suppose was near the centre of the *immense country here called the city*. It is a mile and a half from the President's House, and three miles on a straight line from Georgetown. There is one good tavern about forty rods from the Capitol, and *several other houses are built and erecting;* but I do not perceive how the members of Congress can possibly secure lodgings, unless they will consent to live like scholars in a college or monks in a monastery, crowded ten or twenty in one house, and *utterly secluded from society*. The only resource for such as wish to live comfortably will, I think, be found in Georgetown, three miles distant, *over as bad a road in winter* as the clay grounds near Hartford.

"I have made every exertion to secure good lodgings near the office, but shall be compelled to take them at the distance of more than half a mile. There are, in fact, but *few houses at any one place*, and *most of them small miserable huts*, which present an awful contrast to the public buildings. The people are poor, and, as far as I can judge, they live like fishes, *by eating each other*. All the ground for several miles around the city being, in the opinion of the people, too valuable to be cultivated, remains unfenced. There are but few enclosures, even for gardens, and those are in bad order. You may look in almost any direction, over an extent of ground nearly as large as the city of New York, without seeing a fence or any object except brick-kilns and temporary huts for laborers. * * * Greenleaf's Point presents the appearance of a considerable town which had been destroyed by some unusual calamity. There are [at Greenleaf's Point] fifty or sixty spacious houses, five or six of which are occupied by negroes and vagrants, and a few more by decent looking people; but there are no fences, gardens, nor the least appearance of business. This place is about a mile and a half south of the Capitol."

President Adams (the elder) arrived with his family in November of the same year. On the 25th of that month Mrs. Adams wrote to her daughter, Mrs. Smith, as follows:

"I arrived here on Sunday last, and without meeting with any accident worth noticing, except *losing ourselves* when we left Baltimore, and *going eight or nine miles on the Frederick road*, by which means we were obliged to go the other eight *through the woods*, where we wandered two hours without finding a guide or the path. Fortunately a straggling black came up with us, and we engaged him as a guide to extricate us out of our difficulty; but woods are all you see from Baltimore until you reach *the city*, which is only so in name. Here and there is a small cot, without a glass window, interspersed amongst the forests, through which you travel miles without seeing any human being. In the city there are buildings enough, if they were compact and finished, to accommodate Congress and those attached to it; but as they are, and scattered as they are, I see no great comfort for them. * *

"The house [President's] is upon a grand and superb scale, requiring about thirty servants to attend and keep the apartments in proper order, and perform the ordinary business of the house and stables—an establishment very well proportioned to the President's salary. The lighting the apartments, from the kitchen to parlors and chambers, is a tax indeed, and the fires we are obliged to keep to secure us from daily agues is another very cheering comfort. To assist us in this great castle and render less attendance necessary bells are wholly wanting, not one single one being hung through the whole house, and promises are all you can obtain. This is so great an inconvenience that I know not what to do or how to do. The ladies from Georgetown and in the city have many of them visited me. Yesterday I returned fifteen visits. But such a place as Georgetown appears! Why, our Milton is beautiful. But no comparisons; if they put me up bells and let me have wood enough to keep fires I design *to be pleased*. But, surrounded with forests, can you believe that wood is not to be had, because people cannot be found to cut and cart it. * * * * We have indeed come into a *new country*.

"The house is made habitable, but there is not a single apartment finished, and all within side, except the plastering, has been done since B. came. We have not the *least fence, yard, or convenience without*, and the great unfinished audience-room I make a drying-room of, to hang up the clothes in. * * If the twelve years in which this place has been considered as the future seat of Government had been improved, as they would have been in New England, very many of the present inconveniences would have been removed. It is a beautiful spot, capable of any improvement, and the more I view it the more I am delighted with it."

It must be confessed that the city has not progressed in the rapid ratio which its founders so sanguinely predicted. Although they may not have anticipated anything to compare with the magnificence and luxury which, in many of the European courts, have almost sufficed to build up a city, yet they probably overrated the attractions of the Government and Congress. And these, indeed, are sufficient to have drawn together a much larger population of the retired and wealthy of other cities to reside there, for at least a portion of the year, had Congress complied with its promises, so readily made at is first session, in carrying on a large and judicious system of improvements, so as to have made it a more attractive residence. Had they caused public grounds, connecting the Capitol and President's house, to be planted with trees, and suitably enclosed and protected, instead of confining all their expenditures to the immediate vicinity of the executive and legislative offices, and leaving the remainder a comparative waste, the city would have possessed a much more inviting aspect to strangers; the scattered villages would at this time have been connected by a park, and inducements to build and improve would have been greatly increased.

The following statistics, which we copy from the National Intelligencer of December 12, 1853, will sustain this position. They present a condensed view of the progress of population in the city for the last fifty-three years. The first period includes the members of the Government, clerks and others, who came here with the transfer of the seat of Government, as well as all the artisans and laborers employed on the public grounds:

In 1800	3,210	In 1820	13,474
In 1803	4,332	In 1830	18,831
In 1807	5,652	In 1840	24,300
In 1810	8,208	In 1850	40,001
In 1818	11,499	In 1853	53,000

[The last is an estimated amount probably considerably within the actual population.]

By these tables it will be seen that for the first thirty years the increase of the population was only 15,621, or a fraction more than 520 souls *per annum*. In the next ten years the rate of increase was a fraction less than 567 *per annum*. From 1840 to 1850 the increase, in round numbers, was 15,500, or at the average rate of 1,550 *per annum;* and in the last *three* years the increase has been 13,000, or at the rate of 4,333 and a fraction *per annum*. Taking the last thirteen years together, the increase has been 28,500, or at the average rate of 2,192 and a fraction. So that the increase of the last *thirteen* years amounts to more than the whole increase of the first *forty* years.*

* In the census of 1850, the ratio of increase in the District since 1840 is 18.24; but the fact of Alexandria having been retroceded since 1840 was apparently not taken into consideration. Deducting the population of Alexandria city and county from the census of 1840, and the increase of the rest of the District is at the rate of nearly thirty-three per cent. According to the valuable and accurate tables prepared by Mr. Sessford, the population had increased ten years since the census of 1850—or ten thousand in two years.

4

"These results," says the Intelligencer, "are so different from any to be found in the progressive growth of other cities that we must naturally look to the operation of some extraordinary cause for their production, having no influence on the natural increase of population in other communities. This cause, we have no doubt, has been the uncertainty so long existing as to the city's being the *permanent* Seat of Government. Having neither commerce nor manufactures to offer as inducements to men of capital, to remove from places of active business to a city depending for its prosperity upon the apparently unsettled will of a majority in Congress, its population of course had no aids to its natural rate of increase; and this for the first forty years was a trifle more than one and a half per cent. For the last eight or ten years all uncertainty as to the permanence of the Seat of Government seems to have been dissipated. The liberality of Congress in the expenditure of money for its improvement has given an impulse to the enterprise of our moneyed citizens; and streets that ten years ago had scarcely houses enough upon them to mark their locality, are now thickly-settled places of business. A new and more tasteful style of architecture has taken the place of the uncouth and inconvenient models of earlier times. The number of large and splendid buildings which have been erected as hotels, refectories, and private mansions, within the last three or four years, has entirely changed the face of the city, and given it an appearance more worthy of its name and more indicative of future grandeur."

Another cause of the slow progress of the city, has been the unfortunate result of one of those lottery schemes, to which it was formerly fashionable to resort for the purpose of erecting public buildings. In this instance, the object was to build a city hall and court-house; but, instead of adding to the funds of the city, a debt of nearly $200,000 was contracted. It may be here remarked, however, that such a building has been partially erected, at an expense of $90,000. The Government has, since the year 1823, occupied about one-half of this edifice for a court-house, and has given $40,000 toward the cost—less than has been appropriated in most other territories for the same purpose. An additional reason, if any were wanting, why the United States should contribute largely to this purpose, is, that a large proportion of the business of the courts, which calls for extra accommodation, grows out of suits in which citizens of other States are concerned, and not of the local business of the place.

But the greatest drawback upon the prosperity of the city, has proceeded from one of those schemes of internal improvement which have involved so many States of this Union, and in which the city was encouraged to embark by the action of Congress. We have seen that the founders of the city counted largely upon the advantages to accrue from the western inland trade with Georgetown and Washington, by a connection between the waters of the Potomac and Ohio rivers; a project which was regarded as easy of execution.

At a day anterior to the cession of this District by the States of Maryland and Virginia, those two States had incorporated a company for the improvement of the river Potomac, in the stock of which General Washington became largely interested. The great object of desire continued to be to achieve this work as far as the town of Cumberland, at the base of the Alleghany Mountains, under the confident belief that when that rich mineral region should be reached, a new and greatly enlarged source of trade would be opened, which could not fail to enrich the three corporations of the District. "The canal was designed to have been constructed of the width of thirty feet, and to the depth of three feet of water; the consummation of which, there is little reason to doubt, was fully within the means of the District, with the aid of Virginia and Maryland."* The subject soon attracted a very general interest, and in November, 1823, a convention of delegates, chosen by people of various counties in Maryland, Virginia, Pennsylvania, Ohio, and by the corporate authorities of the District of Columbia, assembled at Washington. New interests had now been brought into connection with the subject, and the object to be obtained became proportionably enlarged. The attention of the Government was given to the subject, and it came to be considered as important that the work should be enlarged, and extended to the Ohio River, in part by national appropriations. In this light President Monroe esteemed it, and accordingly, in his annual message, in December, 1823, submitted it to the consideration of Congress, as a subject of the highest importance to the general interest. Congress, on the 28th of May, 1828, passed an act subscribing $1,000,000, upon condition that the dimensions of the canal should be enlarged. The canal was to be sixty feet wide, and six feet deep; and the expense of the work, as far as Cumberland, was estimated by United States engineers at over $8,000,000; exceeding the estimated cost on the old plan by more than $5,000,000. The committee, in their report to Congress, February 3d, 1836, from which many of these statements are derived, remark:—"In short, no room was left to doubt but that the Government seriously designed to give its best energies to the entire completion of the work. It was perfectly natural, under the circumstances, that the inhabitants of the District should become deeply interested in the project. The city of Washington subscribed $1,000,000,

* Senate Doc. No. 277, 26th Congress, 1st session, which embodies full particulars relative to the canal.

and Alexandria and Georgetown $250,000 each. They may in truth be regarded as having been stimulated to make these large subscriptions, so much beyond their fiscal means, by the direct action of the Government. Without the consent of the Government, they had no authority to make the subscriptions; and the interest taken by the Government in their becoming subscribers, is sufficiently manifest by the terms of the act of Congress."

The Government was aware of the incapacity of the subscribers to meet the payment of their subscriptions, without contracting a loan; and to enable them to do so, it gave the most unquestioned pledge that the loan, and all interest that might accrue on it, should be paid. It assumed the supervision of its payment. If the Government had continued its countenance to this work; if it had given from time to time, from the public treasury, its aid, as it had done in similar cases, and, as there was every reason to suppose they would have done in this, the stock of the canal would have continued to increase in value, and thus the means have been always in the hands of the District cities to reimburse their debt. An opposite policy, however, prevailed in relation to the connection of Government with internal improvements; some of those high in office, who had most strenuously advocated it at first, having changed their views. Maryland put her shoulder to the wheel, and contracted an enormous debt; but, as usually happens in such works, the estimates were below the actual cost, and the canal did not reach that point which would insure any considerable revenue. So long as there was any prospect of this, the citizens of Washington exerted themselves to the utmost to sustain the burden, by taxing themselves, and borrowing money to pay the interest; by which a large additional debt was added to the already oppressive burden. In this state of things, Congress were moved by the consideration hereinbefore mentioned, and the strong equity growing out of them in favor of the people, who, by the Constitution, are placed under its exclusive guardianship, and who, by its change of policy, were thus "devoted to destruction." The debt of $1,000,000 was assumed by the Government, and the stock of the city taken as security for the repayment.

The aid thus obtained from Congress was very great, although the city was still left in debt to the amount of nearly $800,000, (being for money borrowed to pay interest, and the lottery debt.)

The canal is now completed to Cumberland, and the black diamonds are brought down in considerable quantities; but, as yet, the city of Washington has derived little advantage from it; and, what with the superior facilities for shipping at Alexandria, the enormous cost of the canal, and the railroad competition, it is doubtful whether one-half the sanguine expectations of its projectors will ever be realized.

The question is frequently put, WHY SHOULD CONGRESS TAKE UP SO MUCH TIME IN LEGISLATING FOR THE DISTRICT, AND EXPEND SO MUCH MONEY IN MAKING STREETS, AQUEDUCTS, AND BRIDGES IN WASHINGTON, WHEN THE INHABITANTS OF OTHER PLACES TAX THEMSELVES FOR ALL THESE THINGS? Many persons have the idea that the people of the District are not taxed at all.

As well, in order to justify to their constituents those representatives who have voted for appropriations, as to vindicate the citizens from the imputation of abject dependence, we propose to answer this question as succinctly as possible, and in so doing we shall incidentally set forth some other causes which have retarded its growth, in addition to those already mentioned.

1. First then, for wise reasons, Congress has been constituted the sole Legislature of the District, and surely two or three days each session cannot be considered as too much time to be devoted to the legislation of a population of seventy thousand, constantly on the increase.

The fact is, that, for many years past, scarcely one day in a session has been given to this subject; almost all that has been done, having been in the shape of amendments to the civil and diplomatic appropriation bill. The old Maryland laws still govern, and many of them are antiquated and poorly adapted to the wants of the community. It is with the utmost difficulty that corporate facilities can be obtained for the most essential objects. Chief Justice Cranch, of the Circuit Court, many years ago, compiled a civil, and Mr. Edward Livingston, a criminal code, and these were revised and reported upon by a joint committee of the two houses in 1833, but no action has ever been taken upon the reports. However, it is, perhaps, better to have too little than too much legislation, as is the case in most of the States.

2. In the next place, Washington is unlike all other cities in this respect, that it was planned rather to suit the future wants of the country at large, than the convenience of the resident population. In other cities the population is concentrated in one place, and the expenditures in extending streets are made in proportion as the increase of population requires it. New York, for instance, commenced at the Battery, and has gradually extended up. Had the Dutch burghers been required to open streets to Union square, when the population were all concentrated below the City Hall, it would have been thought a very unreasonable requirement. And yet, the proper connexion of the Capitol with the Navy Yard, President's house, Georgetown, and the Arsenal, required in Washington the opening of many miles of connecting streets, when the population consisted of only four or five thousand. This subject was very fully considered by the Hon. Samuel L. Southard, in a report

made to the Senate on the 2d February, 1835, and sustained by letters of Mr. Jefferson, and others, appended thereto.* He remarks: "The plan of the city is one of unusual magnitude and extent; the avenues and streets are very wide, and, for the number of the inhabitants, much greater in distance than those of any other city on this continent, and necessarily require a proportionate expenditure to make and keep them in repair; and, as the city has not grown in the usual manner, but has necessarily been created in a short space of time, the pressure for the public improvements has been alike sudden and burdensome. No people who anticipated the execution and subsequent support of it out of their own funds, would ever have dreamed of forming such a plan."

It is in fact a plan calculated for the magnificent capital of a great nation, but oppressive, from its very dimensions and arrangements, to the inhabitants, if its execution, to any considerable extent, is to be thrown upon them. The expense should at least be joint. This is more especially true in regard to the great avenues; the main object of which was to minister to national pride, by connecting the public edifices with streets worthy the nation.

3. A fund for these improvements has been partly provided out of city lots. The proprietors of the land conveyed the whole of it to Government for the purpose of establishing thereon a national city, according to such plan as the President might adopt. A plan was accordingly made by Government, without consultation with the settlers, creating avenues and streets 100 to 160 feet wide, and embracing an area of 7,134 acres. Of these 7,134 acres, Government retained as reservations 4,118 for streets, avenues, etc.; paid the proprietors but for 512, at the rate of £25 per acre, and returned to them half of the building-lots, (1,058 acres;) thus keeping 5,114 acres as a free gift; *the proceeds of the sales of which building-lots, it was by the deed of cession agreed, should be applied towards the improvement of the place—in grading and making streets, erecting bridges, and providing such other conveniences as the residence of the Government required.* The right of soil in the streets was exclusively vested in the Government, and it was but a fair and reasonable presumption that the Government would bear a large portion of the expense of opening them. Up to the year 1854, about $800,000 had been received from sales of lots. A much larger sum might have been received, had the lots been sold in less haste, and not in so great numbers. Much the larger number were disposed of prior to 1794; and the interest ought to be added up to the time of each appropriation for the streets and avenues, in order to arrive at a

* 23d Congress, 2d session.

correct estimate of the amount due from Government on this account, which would make it nearly double that amount. Seventy thousand dollars in lots has been given to colleges and charitable institutions, fifty thousand dollars of which was to colleges out of the city.

4. The citizens have taxed themselves to the highest limit allowed by law, in order to bear their proportion of the expenses.

From the manner in which assessments are made, this tax (seventy-five cents on the $100, exclusive of special taxes for pumps, gas, pavements, etc.,) is as heavy as that of any other city in the Union, while from the manner in which it is necessarily expended, the return in the shape of benefits is much more indirect. Since it was incorporaed in the year 1802, up to 1854 there had been opened, graded, and improved, about forty miles of streets, costing an outlay of about $600,000; and there had been laid down about 3,000,000 superficial feet of brick pavement, about 25,000 feet of flag-footways, and numerous bridges and culverts erected, (including all the iron bridges across the canal.) More than two hundred thousand dollars have been expended on the canal through the city, concerning which it may be remarked that, whatever Government has contributed in addition to the foregoing, has been fully returned in the facilities furnished for transportation, without toll, of materials and coal to the public buildings and the navy yard, advantages which will be more fully appreciated hereafter. The expense of the pavements is defrayed by a special tax on the property bordering on them; and the streets, bridges, etc., by a tax on the property of the inhabitants generally. For the execution of all these works of improvement, and for the support of the poor and infirm, and the support of public schools, (which have received no grants of lands, such as have been given to other territories,) the inhabitants have been taxed to an aggregate amount of over $3,000,000. A better estimate of what the citizens have done can be formed from the fact, that the following are the only streets which have, to any considerable extent, been improved by the Government: Pennsylvania, New Jersey, Indiana, and Maryland avenues, and Four-and-a-half street.

5. The Government pays no taxes, and it is therefore no more than proper that it should contribute something towards the support of the police and watch of the city, and the lighting and paving of the streets, which pass around its own property, which amounts to nearly as much as the private property. Had it paid taxes, the aggregate would have amounted to more than $2,500,000.

In Mr. Southard's report, it is remarked that "in several States of the Union where the Government holds landed estate, it has paid taxes upon it, and these taxes have been expended for the ordinary municipal purposes of the places where the property was situated. In the acts of incorporation, which give to the city of Washington a partial control and regulation over the streets, there is no exemption of the property of the Government from taxation; and it might, perhaps, be properly inferred that Congress did not intend that it should be exempted, but that it should be equally subject to those burdens which became necessary for the common benefit of the whole. But the corporate authorities have, with prudence and propriety, abstained from levying taxes upon it, and have laid the whole weight upon that part of the property which belonged to individuals, while the Government has been equally participant in the benefits which have resulted from them. * * * The committee are not willing to recommend that there should be any change in this respect; but they believe that provisions should be made by which mutual benefits should be met by mutual burdens, without attempting to decide this question."

Whether it would be expedient, or consistent with the dignity of the nation, to place itself in the position of a tax-payer, may perhaps admit of doubt; but it is no answer to say that, had the Government selected any other city for its residence, public buildings would have been provided, and many other sacrifices cheerfully incurred, for the sake of the benefits which would be thus conferred on the place, without any thought of taxation; for assuming this to be true, other places would have it in their power to confine their expenditures within the space actually occupied; while the accommodations given to Government, however liberal, would, in most instances, be such as not to interfere with, but rather conform to the convenience of the inhabitants—whereas this city was laid out, in the first instance, for the *sole convenience of the Government;* and hence, not only are the inhabitants burdened, in the way we have mentioned, with many useless and unnecessarily wide streets, but the public buildings, being scattered over a wide space, the city has grown up in separate villages around these edifices, and made it necessary to open and improve numbers of connecting streets, before there were inhabitants enough upon them to justify the expense. Besides, would other cities be willing to give up the exclusive jurisdiction to Congress, which experience has shown to be so essential, to secure equal privileges to all sections. But we will hazard the assertion that no city could have furnished such accommodations as the Government required in the way of buildings, certainly they could not have left as extensive reservations for the future wants of Government as are here furnished.

The amount of the canal debt assumed by Congress ($1,000,000) should not be charged against the city, because it was a measure in which, as we have heretofore shown, it embarked on the invitation, as it were, of Congress. It was, in fact, a national undertaking, and had not every reason been given to suppose the nation would do its part, the corporate authorities would never have embarked in it. But, putting this with the interest paid since its assumption, (that paid prior to the assumption the city is still indebted for,) and other appropriations for bridges across the Potomac, etc., not properly chargeable, into the account, we have for all the city appropriations since the city was established, say $3,000,000, which is a liberal estimate. Deducting from this the amount paid into the treasury on account of city lots, with interest, amounting to at least $1,200,000, and we leave $1,800,000, which, in consideration of what we have above stated with regard to the entire absence from taxation, does not seem to be such an extravagant amount. In fact, we think it leaves the United States decidedly on the debtor side.

And here we will remark, that much more might have been accomplished with the same amount of money, had Congress adopted any regular system. In the first place, they have not confided sufficient power to the city corporation to levy taxes for the improvement of the place, for lighting and paving the streets; and a few narrow-minded individuals in a single block may sometimes prevent a measure of the utmost public necessity. In the next place, there has been no division of duty between the corporation and the Government. Appropriations of one often clash with those of the other; and works commenced under an appropriation by Congress are allowed to go to ruin, before a sum is set apart with which to complete them. Either the Government should take the sole charge of certain avenues connecting public edifices, or they should vote a certain sum per annum in lieu of taxes, to be expended by the corporation, under direction of the President; or what would be more equitable than all, they should provide that one-half the expense of opening and grading all streets of a width of one hundred or more feet be paid by the Government, in proportion as the work progresses.

6. The great aqueduct which Congress is, we trust, about to complete will, when finished, be, perhaps, a sufficient satisfaction for all obligations of the Government to the city; but it is not purely for the benefit of the people resident here, that so large an undertaking is required. A reference to the plans and early history of the city conclusively show, that the work of supplying water was expected to devolve upon the Government. It could not be expected that the residents should furnish a supply sufficient for the great fountains on the public grounds, and for sprinkling the wide avenues, all designed on a scale for a nation,

rather than a local population. More than one-half the water supplied from any source would be wanted for Government purposes, and the Department wisely determined to provide for the future. As to the cost, it has been greatly over-rated. Lieutenant Meigs sums up the three plans, as follows:

"The aqueduct from Rock creek, complete, to the Capitol, navy yard, and public buildings, including the high service in Georgetown, will cost $1,258,863. Advantages over the others, *cheapness;* supply in winter and spring, 26,732,300 gallons, but liable, in the heats of summer, to be diminished to 9,860,000 gallons.

"The Little Falls work, complete, will cost $1,597,415. Advantages—over the Great Falls project, cheapness; over Rock Creek, steadiness of supply; which, at the above cost, will be 12,000,000 of gallons, to be increased in time, by another pump and wheel, to 18,000,000. Disadvantages—a doubt as to the sufficiency of the water-power for a greater supply than 12,000,000 of gallons, and, by some engineers whom I have consulted, even for this amount in very dry seasons; want of simplicity; use of machinery always, however well constructed, liable to injury and interruption; want of reservoir space for settling the water; liability to interruption, for a time, during floods.

"The Great Falls project will cost, complete, $1,921,244. Constant and everlasting daily supply, 36,015,400 gallons. Advantages—simplicity and durability; perfect security and inexhaustible and unfailing source; lavish use, which can be indulged in in consequence of abundant supply; power of street-washing, cooling the air, and embellishing the city by great fountains; use for driving small machines, lathes, printing presses, and the like; great space for settling and purifying in reservoirs, and great quantity in store for emergencies; small expense of keeping up the works when once established, and consequent low price of water delivered in houses or factories.

"*If the work is delayed by meagre appropriations, its expense will be much increased; and I hope, in that case, not to be held responsible for its cost above my estimate, which is based upon a steady and vigorous prosecution of the work.*"

When the water is once introduced, all citizens who take the water in their houses or factories must expect to pay a reasonable rent or tax, which no doubt will, in time, return interest at least on such part of the cost as is properly chargeable to the city, if not on the whole. The Corporation of Washington will undertake to collect such rent, and out of it to protect the Government from all costs of repairs, &c.

Finally, it is not by what has been done, that the obligations of Congress in this matter are to be determined. If it was good policy to build a city expressly for a Seat of Government, it is policy to do it well; if it was not good policy, it is now too late to undo what we have done. We have started Washington, and expended enough there to make it incumbent upon us to go on with it; if we are to have a national city, let it be worthy of the nation; at all events, let us leave nothing half finished; if we are to expend $5,000,000 on a Capitol, let us make the ground in front to conform in appearance to some degree; if we are to open splendid streets, let us at least complete them so that they shall prove safe promenades, and not, as now, sources of blinding dust. And, after all, the expense is of little real moment. What is an outlay of a few hundred thousand dollars per annum for such a purpose, to the people of the United States? Who is not proud of every public work completed on a scale worthy the nation? When have we heard a complaint from any section of the country, with regard to the appropriations heretofore made for these purposes? Almost every committee of Congress who have had the claims of the District under consideration, have recognized the propriety of such expenditures, on the ground that they were for the benefit of the nation at large. And the same may be said of most of our Presidents. Mr. Jefferson had no scruples when he planted the poplars upon the avenue, or when he desired to bring into the city the water from the falls of the Potomac, in order that a second Croton might everywhere bubble up on the reservations, and along the avenues, in sparkling fountains, instead of the present insignificant little stream which scarcely supplies the fish-pond and jet d'eux of the Capitol. Nor had General Jackson, when he proposed a splendid stone bridge over the Potomac, in place of the present ricketty wooden structure.

More liberal views, as remarked before, are beginning to prevail in Congress. And let us not be understood as in any way assenting to the idea sometimes entertained, that there should be a representative of the District in that body. There have always been a considerable number of members in both branches, who took correct views of their duty towards the Seat of Government, and have successfully carried through measures of great importance. Were there a representative upon whom the duty of watching over the interests of the city devolved, he would be in a measure left to do his work alone; he would oftentimes be a mere politician, and render himself and his cause odious to those who might, under other circumstances, be on his side. Every thing that can keep the violence of party politics out of the place is desirable.

As at present constituted, there are few cities of similar size where, in proportion to the population, the society presents so mixed a character, combined with so much that is really attractive. As in all places where many strangers congregate, there is a peculiar degree of independence in feelings and habits. The citizens unconnected with Government become so accustomed to see the scenes of political strife acted over during each successive administration, that they have mostly acquired a habit of regarding them with comparative indifference; they are consequently peculiarly free from sectional prejudices. The public officers who form that part of the population most seen by a visitor, exhibit in their ranks a singular medley of talent, mediocrity, oddity, and misfortune.

The change which takes place on the approach of a session of Congress, after a long recess, has been most aptly compared to that of a great watering place on the approach of a fashionable season. Then comes the whole coterie of foreigners, gentlemen attracted by curiosity, political demagogues, claimants, patentees, letter writers, army and navy officers, office-hunters, gamblers, and blacklegs. Pennsylvania avenue presents an animated scene in the number of strangers from every section of the country, not excepting a representative or two from the Indian tribes.

All fashions are here in vogue, and a party presents so much variety of character and habit, as to make it peculiarly attractive to a man of the world.

The establishment of the Smithsonian Bequest must tend to draw thither men of science, who will make it their residence throughout the year, give more stability to society, and create an object of interest independent of Government and Congress.

The Washington Monument is slowly but steadily rising from the ground, and is becoming every year more attractive from the interest which is elicited by the manner in which funds are contributed throughout the land, (every one who has given, desiring to look upon the work,) and the sculptured blocks from States and associations.

An Equestrian Statue of Jackson has, also, been reared mostly by private contributions, and the Government has ordered one of Washington by the same artist. It is to be hoped that it will be placed on that part of the mall bounded by Twelfth and Fourteenth streets, between the Smithsonian grounds and the National monument. It will thus have a whole square to itself, and be visible from the Capitol to great advantage; and around it there will be an opportunity for placing some of those other statues which were voted by the old Congress—one to General Greene, for instance.

The triangular spaces which are being enclosed along Pennsylvania avenue, will form appropriate places for pedestrian statues to Clay, Webster, and J. Q. Adams, whose names are not only associated with the country at large, but especially embalmed in the memory of citizens here. But we propose to speak on this subject more at length in another chapter.

There is an impression prevalent abroad that Washington is a very expensive place. These opinions are formed from the cost of boarding houses and hotels, where the charge per diem is regulated very much by the usages of similar establishments in other cities; but it is by housekeeping that the cost of living is to be estimated. The value of land is controlled, and always must be to a greater or less degree, by the wants of those connected with the Government; and rents are consequently lower, so that the majority of clerks can lease and even own property within a reasonable distance of the places of business and fashionable quarters to far greater advantage than they could in the same sections of New York, Philadelphia, and Baltimore. The same causes which produce independence in manners and dress, operate in rngulating the size and finish of a house, its furniture, and style of living, and there is but little inducement to ape one's neighbor simply because "it is the fashion." An examination of the market reports in the public papers will show too that the cost of marketing of all kinds is below the average in other cities; and those officers of Government who complain of the expense of living in Washington, if they compare their statements with those of older clerks, will frequently have the satisfaction of finding that it is their own fault, or the consequence of extravagant habits contracted when in better circumstances elsewhere. We do not mean to assert that the salaries of our public functionaries are in all cases sufficiently high for the style of living they are expected to sustain. A Secretary comes with his family to Washington, takes and furnishes a house, and perhaps before the end of three months a dissolution of the Cabinet renders it necessary to break up his establishment, and sell out at a ruinous loss. It is therefore to be regretted that the plan of providing houses for the members of the Cabinet and foreign ministers has been abandoned. There is no reason why, on the score of convenient access, if for no other reason, the same permanence of location should not be given to the representatives of each department of our Government as to the Chief Magistrate. It is no answer to say that those who hold these stations are not placed there to live handsomely and entertain. So we have heard it said with regard to our foreign ministers, and yet every American who goes abroad expects to make his minister's house to a certain extent his home, and feels mortified if he does not find him in a pleasant and fashionable section. At Washington there is no visitor who does not expect to find a Cabinet minister in something more than a mere boarding-house. He desires to have an opportunity of seeing him out of his office, and in a position at least equal to that of a private gentleman. Besides, it is to them that strangers look for an interchange of that civility and courtesy which our ministers receive abroad. The most ultra-radical in his views cannot but pay some deference to the opinions of the world in these matters; or else, to be consistent, he would, on the same principle, prohibit our national vessels from firing complimentary salutes to those of other nations, because they were supplied with powder for another purpose. To assist the President in dispensing the hospitalities and courtesies of life, is almost as much expected of a Secretary as if it were laid down in his code of duties. It is only necessary that it should continue to be an incidental, and not a main thing, in order to retain it within moderate bounds; and we contend that, owing to the simple standard of living produced by moderate fortunes and constant changes in society, this may be done at Washington at less expense than elsewhere. Even now, a Secretary, with his eight thousand a year, entertains more than a New Yorker with double that sum, though not in the same way, which is not usually expected, since few or none undertake to do so.

Another prevalent impression, to which the writing of Dickens have given currency, and which is revived every time a member dies, is that the national capital is unhealthy. When first laid out there were, as in all newly-settled places, a number of marshes which gave rise to fever and ague, and malarial complaints. But these are being rapidly drained or filled up, and we believe there is no city in the Union where fewer deaths occur in proportion to the population; for, according to the reports of health, the average has been no more than two per day in a population of twenty to twenty-five thousand. The heat of the summer months is peculiarly oppressive in consequence of the width of the streets and the lowness of the houses, but we have not heard any complaint that is not equally common in all the Southern States. It is a fact worthy of note, that out of all those whose names are recorded upon the monuments of the Congressional Cemetery, by far the greater proportion died either by complaints which they brought with them to Washington, or which were caused by their imprudent and irregular habits of life. Indeed, it is a wonder that more do not die, when we consider how entirely their usual course of living is changed. Nothing can be more irregular than the life of a member of Congress. He goes to the Capitol at ten o'clock, is engaged upon committees until twelve, and then passes through the damp passages of that huge mass of stone into the over-heated halls of the Senate or House. Here he remains four, six, or perhaps twelve hours; and, if he is desirous of being present at every call of the yeas and nays, his lunch or dinner must be postponed accordingly; and perhaps that meal will eventually be taken by candle-light, upon invitation, after which the remainder of the evening is spent out at a party. It is obvious what an effect these irregular hours, and the constant display before him of all the luxuries of the season, with wines and liquors, must have upon a man who has always been accustomed at his village home to dine at one upon a single dish.

No wonder that dyspepsia prevails. But this is not all. If at all inclined to dissipation, an easy and pleasant road is opened to him; and not a few yield to the temptation. Every one who has lived in Washington during the last few years, and paid much attention to these matters, will remember many most glaring cases of this kind, for which the climate has been blamed by friends at a distance. On the other hand the place has become a favorite residence to many on account of its being favorable to health.

We have endeavored in the preceding pages to set forth the reasons which led to the selection of Washington as the Seat of Government of the United States, and to show that the force of this reasoning has been illustrated, and the expectation of the founders fully realized in the progress of the city, notwithstanding the defects of the plan, and the absence of any systematic legislation for its benefit.

It never can become a great city in the ordinary sense of the term that is to say, it can never be the seat of a very heavy commerce, and consequently of long rows of warehouses and striking contrasts between the extremes of wealth and poverty; but it may become a place for the cultivation of that political union and that social intercourse which more than anything else unbends the sterner feelings of our nature, and dispels all sectional prejudices. Its prosperity will be no unfit emblem of the progress of our republic, for it is now occupied in about the same proportion with our extended territory; and every sensible increase to the population of the Union, adds a mite to that of this city, since it augments the machinery of Government.

The history of all nations shows that the political capital, even when unaccompanied with great power or splendor, has exercised an important influence over the country. As the seat of all the great events in in its political history, the place where all its discordant spirits meet on common ground, and where all differences are healed; and as the site of most of its monuments to the illustrious dead, new interest is constantly added to the spot, and new ardor awakened for imitating the example of the great and good men whose memory is there preserved; and for the support of those institutions which they handed down. What Englishman does not feel a double attachment to London for its Westminister Abbey and Hall, and their thousand poetical and historical associations? And so of Notre Dame, St. Dennis, and the hundred other edifices rich in the memory of the past at Paris. As the continued contemplation of painting and sculpture cultivates a taste for what is refined, so the silent lesson taught by the presence of such monuments in our midst, conduce in no small degree to temper our reflections, and moderate our actions.

Now to apply these remarks to our own capital. Founded by the illustrious man whose name it bears, it will form his appropriate monument, for here will be presented at one view the operation of those institutions, the establishment of which was in so great a degree his work. Here will be congregated for the greater part of every year many of the ruling minds of the nation, who may be in constant intercourse with the representatives of other lands; and, from this continued mingling of intellects, as well as from official sources, will be collected the most accurate information relative to the commerce, manufactures, agriculture, and mechanical ingenuity of the country. Already do the Patent Office, and the collections of the Exploring Expedition, and other agencies, form a museum far exceeding in interest any other in the country. And does not every year add new interest to that Capitol where already the voice of the sire is re-echoed in the seats of honor occupied by the son; where, with the present facilities of access, every hall, every picture, every statue becomes daily more familiar to the citizens of the most distant State, ministering to a laudable pride in the embellished appearance in this the only Westminister which we can boast, and inspiring a wish to make a goodly building of that framework which our fathers planned.

Some persons entertain a conscientious repugnance to the continuance of slavery on a national territory. One word on that much-vexed question. The last census shows a very considerable decrease in the number of slaves in Maryland and Virginia; and any one who has ever lived in that section for the last few years, must have discovered causes at work, such as the introduction of white labor by New Englanders and Germans, the deterioration of slaves by intercourse with free blacks, etc., which will make it the interest of the inhabitants to get rid of the evil by gradual means.

"You cannot divest slavery, from the influence of certain causes which have heretofore and will continue to operate upon it, producing results beyond the control of human legislation. These have been most ably presented by a citizen of Kentucky of great attainments, John A. McClung, Esq., in a speech delivered before the Kentucky Colonization Society in January last. Our decennial tables of population prove that, in reference to many States in our Union, slavery has been marked by three distinct stages: the first is when the slave population increases at a greater ratio than the white; the second, when the white population increases at a greater ratio than the slave; and the third when the slave population actually decreases. It is remarkable too that these changes have progressed with great regularity, establishing beyond controversy that, when the slave population begins to decrease, it must go on until the causes which produced its decline will ultimately exterminate it. New York and New Jersey together had, in 1790, 32,747 slaves. By the census of 1800 the number of slaves in these two States had increased only eighteen; but there was a decrease in New York of 981, and an increase in New Jersey of 999. After 1800 the slaves in both States rapidly declined, until in 1840 there were but 678 left, and now in both States the institution has been abolished. In Delaware the number of slaves has decreased from 8,887 in 1790 to 2,605 in 1840. In Maryland the number of slaves increased until 1810. In 1820 they had decreased from 111,502 to 107,398. Thus the number for a period of ten years fell about 4,000. In the next period of ten years the fall was a little more than 5,000, and by the census of 1840 the number had come down to 89,737, exhibiting a diminution in number of 12,457 in the last ten years. In the District of Columbia the number of slaves was 6,377 in 1820, had slightly declined in 1830, and came down to 4,694 in 1840. In Virginia the number of slaves continued to increase until 1830, when they reached 469,757. The census of 1840 exhibits a decline of 20,770. Thus we see that slavery has reached its height in the States on the Atlantic, including Virginia and all north and east, and commenced declining, making such progress that those farthest north and east have abolished the institution."*

In 1850 the number of slaves in the District, had decreased to 3,687.

In relation to the proposition for abolishing slavery here there are two considerations not usually regarded sufficiently in discussing the subject:

First. Under any circumstances so long as slavery exists in any part of the country there will always be some slaves at the Seat of Government, wherever it may be. It is, under the Constitution, a kind of neutral ground, where all sections and parties have a right to meet on equal terms, and those who come from the South, whether as members of Congress or as public functionaries, may claim, with much reason, a right to hold slaves during their sojourn.

Secondly. Were slavery abolished, the present Seat of Government, surrounded as it is by slave States, would become at once a place of refuge for fugitive slaves from the adjoining States. It would become a perfect negro hunting ground for slave owners and those who are tempted by rewards offered for the re-capture of fugitives. There would be constant demands on the United States Executive for the surrender of these fugitives. Those at the North who have had occasion to observe the difficulties and embarrassment which have attended the execution of the fugitive law, can appreciate the difficulties in which a Northern Presi-

---

***From a Speech of Mr. Senator Underwood, of Kentucky.**

dent would be placed when daily and almost hourly called upon to deliver up these poor captives. The sight of them, returning to a bondage, perhaps more severe, or sold, for their offence, to the Georgia plantations, would be perhaps a more humiliating spectacle from the Capitol than that which was presented before the abolition of the slave trade. To the citizens of the District it would be a serious evil to have these poor creatures concealed in great numbers in the city, only venturing out in the night time, and driven by destitution and suffering to the most desperate undertakings.

We have seen that some of the slave States, in their conventions for ratifying the Federal Constitution, expressed serious apprehensions lest the article about the "ten miles square" should open the way at some future time, for an asylnm for fugitives from the States, and the fear seems to have been allayed, and the article acceded to, by reason of the assurances given by those who had been members of the National Convention, and by the articles in the Federalist, that there would be a local government, invested with the control of all matters in which the security and protection of Congress was not involved. This fact furnishes a reason why Congress should not act in this matter without some little deference to the effect which their legislation might have on the adjoining States.

Indeed, since the abolition of the slave trade under the Compromise measures, no very strong demonstration in favor of such a movement has been made, and all reflecting persons will see the propriety of letting the question alone.

As we have given an account of the ceremony of laying the first corner-stone of the Capitol by Washington, we cannot better close our history, than by giving an extract from Mr. Webster's address, on the occasion of the laying of the corner-stone of the Capitol extension, by President Fillmore, on the 4th of July, 1851.*

"FELLOW CITIZENS: By the act of Congress of 30th September, 1850, provision was made for the extension of the Capitol, according to such plan as might be approved by the President of the United States. This measure was imperatively demanded for the use of the Legislative and Judiciary departments, the public libraries, the occasional accommodation of the Chief Executive Magistrate, and for other objects. No act of Congress incurring a large expenditure has received more general approbation from the people. The President has proceeded to execute this law. He has approved a plan; he has appointed an architect; and all things are now ready for the commencement of the work.

*The area of the Capitol of 1793 was one-half acre; with the extension it will cover four and one-third acres.

"The anniversary of National Independence appeared to afford an auspicious occasion for laying the foundation-stone of the additional building. That ceremony has now been performed, by the President himself, in the presence and view of this multitude. He has thought that the day and the occasion made a united and imperative call for some short address to the people here assembled; and it is at his request that I have appeared before you to perform that part of the duty which was deemed incumbent on us.

"Beneath the stone is deposited, among other things, the following brief account of the proceedings of this day, in my handwriting:

'On the morning of the first day of the seventy-sixth year of the Independence of the United States of America, in the City of Washington, being the 4th day of July, 1851, this stone, designed as the corner-stone of the extension of the Capitol, according to a plan approved by the President, in pursuance of an act of Congress, was laid by

MILLARD FILLMORE,

PRESIDENT OF THE UNITED STATES,

assisted by the Grand Master of the Masonic Lodges, in the presence of many members of Congress, of officers of the Executive aud Judiciary Departments, National, State, and District, of officers of the Army and Navy, the Corporate authorities of this and neighboring cities, many associations, civil and military and masonic, officers of the Smithsonian Institution and National Institute, professors of colleges and teachers of schools of the District, with their students and pupils, and a vast concourse of people from places near and remote, including a few surviving gentlemen who witnessed the laying of the corner-stone of the Capitol by President Washington, on the eighteenth day of September, seventeen hundred and ninety-three.

"If, therefore, it shall be hereafter the will of God that this structure shall fall from its base, that its foundation be upturned, and this deposit brought to the eyes of men, be it then known, that, on this day, the Union of the United States of America stands firm, that their Constitution still exists unimpaired, and with all its original usefulness and glory; growing every day stronger and stronger in the affections of the great body of the American people, and attracting more and more the admiration of the world. And all here assembled, whether belonging to public life or to private life, with hearts devoutly thankful to Almighty God for the preservation of the liberty and happiness of the country, unite in sincere and fervent prayers that this deposit, and the walls and arches, the domes and towers, the columns and entablatures now to be erected over it may endure forever!

'God save the United States of America.

'DANIEL WEBSTER,

'*Secretary of State of the United States.*'

"Fellow-citizens: Fifty-eight years ago Washington stood on this spot to execute a duty like that which has now been performed. He then laid the corner-stone of the original Capitol. He was at the head of the Government, at that time weak in resources, burdened with debt, just struggling into political existence and respectability, and agitated by the heaving waves which were overturning European thrones. But even then, in many important respects, the Government was strong. It was strong in Washington's own great character; it was strong in the wisdom and patriotism of other eminent public men, his political associates and fellow-laborers; and it was strong in the affections of the people.

"Since that time astonishing changes have been wrought in the condition and prospects of the American People; and a degree of progress witnessed with which the world can furnish no parallel. As we review the course of that progress, wonder and amazement arrest our attention at every step. * * * * * * * * *

"Who does not admit that this unparalleled growth in prosperity and renown is the result, under Providence, of the Union of these States, under a general Constitution, which guaranties to each State a republican form of Government, and to every man the enjoyment of life, liberty, and the pursuit of happiness, free from civil tyranny or ecclesiastical domination?

"And to bring home this idea to the present occasion, who does not feel that, when President Washington laid his hand on the foundation of the first Capitol building, he performed a great work of perpetuation of the Union and the Constitution? Who does not feel that this seat of the General Government, heathful in its situation, central in its poition, near the mountains from whence gush springs of wonderful virtue, teeming with Nature's richest products, and yet not far from the bays and the great estuaries of the sea, easily accessible and generally agreeable in climate and association, does give strength to the Union of these States; that this city, bearing an immortal name, with its broad streets and avenues, its public squares and magnificent edifices of the general Government, erected for the purposes of carrying on within them the important business of the several Departments; for the reception of wonderful and curious inventions, the preservation of the records of American learning and genius; of extensive collections of the products of nature and art, brought hither for study and comparison from all parts of the world; adorned with numerous churches, and sprinkled over, I am happy to say, with many public schools, where all children of the city, without distinction, are provided with the means of obtaining a good education; where there are academies and colleges, professional schools and public libraries, should continue to receive, as it has heretofore received, the fostering care of Congress, and should be regarded as the permanent seat of the National Government. Here, too, a citizen of the great republic of letters, a republic which knows not the metes and bounds of political geography, has prophetically indicated his conviction that America is to exercise a wide and powerful influence in the intellectual world, by founding in this city, as a commanding position in the field of science and literature, and placing under the guardianship of the Government, an institution 'for the increase and diffusion of knowledge among men.'

"With each succeeding year new interest is added to the spot; it becomes connected with all the historical associations of our country, with her statesmen and her orators, and, alas! its cemetery is annually enriched with the ashes of her chosen sons.

"Before us is the broad and beautiful river, separating two of the original thirteen States, and which a late President, a man of determined purpose and inflexible will, but patriotic heart, desired to span with arches of ever-enduring granite, symbolical of the firmly cemented union of the North and the South. That President was General Jackson.

"On its banks repose the ashes of the Father of his Country, and at our side, by a singular felicity of position, overlooking the city which he designed, and which bears his name, rises to his memory the marble column, sublime in its simple grandeur, and fitly intended to reach a loftier height than any similar structure on the surface of the whole earth.

"Let the votive offerings of his grateful countrymen be freely contributed to carry higher and still higher this monument. May I say, as on another occasion, 'Let it rise; let it rise, till it meet the sun in his coming; let the earliest light of the morning gild it, and parting day linger and play on its sbmmit!'

"Fellow-citizens, what contemplations are awakened in our minds as we assemble here to re-enact a scene like that performed by WASHINGTON! Methinks I see his venerable form now before me, as presented in the glorious statue by Houdon, now in the Capitol of Virginia. He is dignified and grave; but concern and anxiety seem to soften the lineaments of his countenance. The Government over which he presides is yet in the crisis of experiment. Not free from troubles at home, he sees the world in commotion and in arms all around him. He sees that imposing foreign Powers are half disposed to try the strength of the recently-established American Government. We perceive that mighty thoughts, mingled with fears as well as with hopes, are struggling within him. He heads a short procession over these then naked fields; he crosses yonder stream on a fallen tree; he ascends to the top of this eminence, whose original oaks of the forest stand as thick around him as if the spot had been devoted to Druidical worship, and here he performs the appointed duty of the day.

"And now, fellow-citizens, if this vision were a reality; if Washington actually were now amongst us, and if he could draw around him the shades of the great public men of his own days, patriots and warriors, orators and statesmen, and were to address us in their presence, would he not say to us, 'Ye men of this generation, I rejoice and thank God for being able to see that our labors and toils and sacrifices were not in vain. You are prosperous, you are happy, you are grateful; the fire of liberty burns brightly and steadily in your hearts, while DUTY and the LAW restrain it from bursting forth in wild and destructive conflagration. Cherish liberty, as you love it; cherish its securities as you wish to preserve it. Maintain the Constitution which we labored so painfully to establish, and which has been to you such a source of inestimable blessings. Preserve the union of the States, cemented as it was by our prayers, our tears, and our blood. Be true to God, to your country, and to your duty. So shall the whole Eastern World follow the morning sun to contemplate you as a nation; so shall all generations honor you, as they honor us; and so shall that Almighty Power which so graciously protected us, and which now protects you, shower its everlasting blessings upon you and your posterity.'

* * * * * * * * * *

"President Fillmore, it is your singularly good fortune to perform an act such as that which the earliest of your predecessors performed fifty-eight years ago. You stand where he stood; you lay your hand on the corner-stone of a building designed greatly to extend that whose corner-stone he laid. Changed, changed is every thing around. The same sun, indeed, shone upon his head which now shines upon yours. The same broad river rolled at his feet, and bathes his last resting place, that now rolls at yours. But the site of this city was then mainly an open field. Streets and avenues have since been laid out and completed, squares and public grounds enclosed and ornamented, until the city which bears his name, although comparatively inconsiderable in numbers and wealth, has become quite fit to be the seat of government of a great and united people.

"Sir, may the consequences of the duty which you perform so auspiciously to day equal those which flowed from his act."

NOTE.—We should have noted, in the proper place, the obligations citizens are under to W. W. Corcoran, Esq., Secretary Henry, and Mayor Lenox, for their efforts in bringing about the action of Congress, and of the President, towards securing the improvement of the public grounds, and the invaluable services of the lamented Downing.

CHAPTER IV.

MONUMENTAL STRUCTURES.

CUI BONO? THEIR INFLUENCE—THOSE ERECTED BY VOLUNTARY CONTRIBUTION OF MOST VALUE—MONUMENTS IN EUROPE—ACTION OF CONTINENTAL CONGRESS—MONUMENT TO GENERAL GREENE—TO GENERAL MONTGOMERY—PROVISION FOR MONUMENTS AT THE FEDERAL CITY—CONGRESSIONAL CEMETERY—RESOLUTIONS OF 1783—RESOLUTION TO REMOVE THE BODY OF WASHINGTON TO CAPITOL—PROPOSED MAUSOLEUM—ACTION OF VIRGINIA—PURCHASE OF MOUNT VERNON—GREENOUGH'S STATUE—EQUESTRIAN STATUE ORDERED—MR. MACON'S REMARKS—OTHER MONUMENTS—NATIONAL MONUMENT PROJECTED—HOW TO RAISE THE FUNDS—PRESENTATION BLOCKS—PLANS—MATERIAL.

Public attention has so frequently been called during the last few years to the progress of the Washington National Monument, that a few remarks and facts on the subject of that, and monumental structures in general, may not be without interest.

Cui-bono? is the question which many a plodding business man has propounded, when a subscription paper for some such object has been presented to him.

Monuments are useless structures we are told. Those men who do not live in history deserve no monument, and those whose deeds are there recorded need none.

The first part of the proposition is not strictly true, for there are many philanthropists, public benefactors, and inventors, who occupy but a small space in history by the side of kings, generals, and statesmen, who produced greater sensation at the time they lived.

The works of Howard, Watt, Fulton, and Whitney, live after them, but the crowd who enjoy the benefit of their labors seldom have their attention called to the names which are to be cherished in memory in connection therewith. But admitting the first position to be true, the second one is by no means so clear. In the first place, if you take the mass of mankind, you find but a small number comparatively who read books of any kind, especially history, and, of those who do read, comparatively few preserve a distinct recollection of prominent characters and leading events. Upon such persons objects presented to the senses make the greatest impression, and a monument or painting lead to inquiry and keep the subject constantly before the mind. They naturally feel that they ought to know something about an event or individual deemed worthy of such a memento; and pride of country at least stimulates us to avoid appearing ignorant on the subject commemorated. Who that passes the Battle Monument in Baltimore does not endeavor to brush up his memory concerning the contest at North Point; so of the Naval Monument and the sculpture and paintings in the rotunda of the Capitol at Washington; would not one who had been in the habit of passing there for weeks together feel ashamed not to know something of the events and persons referred to? You may see on almost any pleasant day, one or more persons reading the inscription on the tall monument to Emmett in St. Paul's church-yard, New York, and many an Irishman has thus been informed for the first time of the history of his eminent countryman. So, at the entrance of Trinity church-yard, the "Dont give up the ship," on Capt. Lawrence's tomb stone, arrests attention and refreshes the memory of the visitor upon the achivements of our little navy during the late war.

But, in the next place, it is a mistake to suppose that the chief object of a monument is to preserve the memory of an individual. Is it not rather an evidence of the value set upon the deceased by those who reared the Obelisk, a testimonial of the appreciation of him by those survived? We place a marble tablet over a father's grave, not because we fear that we shall forget him; but because we desire, and the world expects us to testify our respect for him by some such visible sign.

The best evidence of patriotism is a disposition to make some sacrifices for the cause we believe to be just; and so the best evidence of gratitude is some voluntary offering from our treasures, something more than the mere empty thanks which cost no individual effort to bestow them.

Hence the monuments which are by far the most interesting in their associations, are those which have been erected by voluntary contributions, not by a mere appropriation from the public treasury, which, though all are taxed for it, no one feels; but by some little personal sacrifice. A mere pile of rude stones, each of which is brought by a different individual, as is said to be the case with many Indian monuments, speaks much more forcibly of the respect entertained for the dead than a gorgeous pillar built by the decree of a parliament or the will of a ruler.

This furnishes a reply to those who ask with reference to the Washington National Monument, why not let Congress complete it by a sweeping appropriation out of our overflowing treasury, and thus end the matter. Such an appropriation would soon send up the shaft, but the visitor would not look on it with half the interest he now feels, when he reflects, that for every stone, one or more individuals have voluntarily brought forward their contributions.

Every city in Europe is filled with monuments; but very few of them are the work of popular enthusiasm, or commemorate anything more than a royal visit, or an exalted rank, monuments erected by town councils or the owners of property around particular parks, as acts of civility, sometimes of servility.

There are in London some thirteen statues of sovereigns—four of the brothers of sovereigns, four generals, and one philanthropist.

The costly column to the Duke of York is jeered at, because public sentiment would never have built what parliament voted in deference to a king's brother. Of course we do not mean to say that this is the case with all such structures reared by parliamentary grants. Nelson's and Wellington's monuments are among the exceptions.* And there are

* "The moral power of example is stronger than numbers. England understands how much national pride and patriotism are kept alive by paintings of her great events, and monuments raised over her dead. I have seen the Duke of Wellington reining his steed past his own colossal statue, melted from the cannon he himself took in battle, reared to him by a grateful country before he died. London has her Trafalgar-square, and a glorious monument to Nelson. Whenever an English patriot falls, England calls on art to commemorate the spot; so does France; so has Italy in all ages. Kings and statesmen have understood how much national existence depends on national pride and patriotism; and how much also *those* depend on monuments and mementos of her great dead. The palace of Versailles is filled with paintings of Napoleon's great battles. * * * The countries of the old world are covered with paintings and monuments to those who fell in a less worthy cause than freedom. But where are the monuments to Allen, and Starke, and Putnam, and Warren, and Perry, and McDonough, Decatur, and Lawrence? Young Hale was sent as a spy by Washington into the enemy's camp. Being discovered, he was hung on a gallows, and met his fate with the lofty enthusiasm and courage of a Spartan hero. He laid down his young life without a murmur for his country. But who can tell where he sleeps? His country in her hour of darkness and bitter need, asked for his life, and he gave it without a sigh; and now that country dishonors his grave. Yet Andre has a monument in the heart of the British Empire. The youth of every land are educated more by art than by speeches. Let monuments rise from Concord, Lexington, Bennington, Ticonderoga, Yorktown, and Plattsburgh, and Chippewa, and Lundy's Lane, and New Orleans, and as the rail car flies over the country, let these records of our struggles and our victories come and go on the hasty traveller, and noble thoughts and purposes will mingle in the headlong excitement after gain. Let the statues of the signers of the Declaration of Independence line Pennsylvania Avenue, and he who walks between them to the Capitol will be a better man and better patriot. Let great paintings, illustrating our chequered, yet most instructive history, fill our public galleries, and when the country wants martyrs they will be ready."—*From Headley's Address to the Art Union.*

In a speech of Mr. Smith, of Alabama, in relation to Kossuth, the failure of all attempts at republicanism in Europe, is ascribed in part to "their antiquities and their monuments, breathing, smacking, and smelling of nobility and royalty," concerning which, Greenough in his Æsthetics in Washington thus remarks:

"I rejoice to find that American Legislators have found out the value and significance of monuments and of antiquities in their political influence. May we not expect that our civilization and our institutions will obtain this support from Congress? * * * I will now merely state that there stands in the studio of Mr. Powers, at Florence, a statue of America, which is not only a beautiful work of art, but which "breaths, smacks, and smells" of Republicanism and Union. If placed conspicuously by Mr. Walter, in one of the new wings of the Capitol, it would be a monument of union. The sooner it is done the sooner it will become an 'antiquity.'"

some which are more appropriately the work of the legislature. Such are those which are intended to mark particular spots, battle-fields for instance. It is of the greatest advantage to the visitor to have, upon some small structure, a concise and accurate account of the event which occurred, and the absence of such memorials at Saratoga, Lake George, Lundy's Lane, Yorktown and other places of interest is to be regretted. As they are for convenience rather than to testify the sentiments of those who erected them, the public treasury is almost the only source from which the funds are to be derived.

Were there no monuments but such as are erected by voluntary contributions, there would be very few indeed; but those few would be real evidence of merit.

Many monuments in Europe were reared by the individuals they were intended to honor. Napoleon was not at all modest in this respect; but such was his real greatness that he could afford to do what others could not. Besides, his monuments commemorate others besides himself—great events, great generals, brave legions. He knew well how to minister to the pride of the soldier, and excite a thirst for glory. His noblest monuments are the splendid bridges and elegant edifices he built in various parts of his empire. But the effect his triumphal arches have had on the soldiery is sufficient evidence that monuments exercise no small influence. History is full of such evidence.

The Continental Congress seems to have considered a monument as the only appropriate testimonial of respect to a great man, and voted one where we should now present a sword or a gold medal. After the battle of Eutaw Springs, a resolution was passed directing one to be erected to General Greene, at the future Seat of Government. This has never been built. In this connection we may mention, that the cannon taken in the battle were presented to him on that occasion, and were appropriately inscribed. General Greene died three years after the war, leaving a family of young children, and an estate embarrassed by the noble efforts he had made to clothe and feed his destitute army. Under such circumstances the attention of his widow was given to more immediate duties, and, though the medal of the Eutaws and other reliques were religiously gathered under the family roof, these bulky cannon were allowed to remain at West Point, where they would be better preserved than in a private house; and it is well they were not removed to the General's residence, as in that case they would have fallen into the hands of their original owners, Admiral Cockburn having made this house his headquarters for several weeks during the last war. The cannon are still to be seen at West Point, and, should the resolution of Congress be ever carried into effect, they would form a beautiful and appropriate accompaniment to the monument. The family are willing to place them at the disposal of Government for that purpose.

On a neat tablet in front of St. Paul's Church, New York, is the following inscription:

"*This monument is erected by order of Congress,* 25*th January,* 1776, *to transmit to posterity a grateful remembrance of the patriotism, conduct, enterprise and perseverence of Major General Richard Montgomery, who, after a series of successes amidst the most disarming difficulties, fell in the attack on Quebec,* 31 *December,* 1775, *aged* 37 *years.*"

On a stone beneath is the following:

"*The State of New York caused the remains of Major General Richard Montgomery to be conveyed from Quebecc, and deposited beneath this monument the* 8*th day of July,* 1818."

As indicative of the public sentiment fifty years ago, we may mention that one of the finest squares in the Federal city (that now occupied by the Patent Office) was reserved by the Commissioners for a National Church, in which to hold services of public thanksgiving, and as an appropriate receptacle for the monuments which Congress might erect to the heroes of the Revolution, or other benefactors. Fifteen squares were to be divided among the several States, to be adorned and improved, and receive monuments of celebrated citizens of the States.

These suggestions of the Commissioners have never been carried out, though they appear to have met with general approval at the time. The only place at Washington, besides the Capitol, where monuments have been erected by Congress, is the Eastern Burial Ground, more generally known as the Congressional Cemetery. It is not, as has been supposed, public property, by far the greater portion being taken up with private burial lots. The only privilege the Government possesses is, that of erecting monuments or burying at a certain fixed price.*

Over the graves of Vice President Gerry and Major General Brown are handsome marble monuments, but we remember no other memorial erected by Congress, unless we are to dignify with this name that square, tasteless mass of free-stone which, under some standing law or rule, is erected for every member of Congress who happens to die in Washington, whether buried there or not. They are all exactly alike, with the same official inscription, as for example: "Hon. John Quincy Adams, a representative in Congress, from the State of Massachusetts, who died on the —— day of February."†

* The amount received from this Cemetery is understood to be ample for all desirable improvements, but is applied, in part, to the support of the church to which it belongs. Could not a company be formed to buy it out?

† There is a handsome monument to Vice President Clinton, erected by his children.

An effort was made at the time of Mr. Adams' death to have this altered, so that a monument more befitting an ex-President should be erected; but it was voted down, chiefly from a feeling that it might be an unwise precedent to erect special monuments where the parties were buried elsewhere. The same sentiments doubtless influenced the rejection of the Senate bill for a monument to General Taylor. It would seem that it were wiser to abolish the present practice altogether, except where members are buried at Washington, which is rarely the case; or, if it is to be continued, then there might be at least a more tasteful block devised, and sufficient variety obtained by giving to each State a particular form, to answer on all future occasions. The delegates of each State might be allowed to decide upon this, and when a member dies, his colleagues might designate some one of their number to prepare a suitable inscription, on their neglect to do which within a given time, the ordinary official title might be cut upon the stone.

In 1783 Congress passed the following resolutions:

"*Resolved unanimously, (ten States being present,) That an equestrian statue of General Washington be erected at the place where the residence of Congress shall be established.*

"*Resolved, That the statue be of bronze, the General to be represented in a Roman dress, holding a truncheon in his right hand, and his head encircled with a laurel wreath; the statue to be supported by a marble pedestal, on which are to be represented, in bas relief, the following principal events of the war in which General Washington commanded in person, namely, the evacuation of Boston; the capture of the Hessians at Trenton; the battle of Princeton; the action of Monmouth; and the surrender of York. On the upper part of the front of the pedestal to be engraved as follows:*

"'*The United States in Congress assembled ordered this statue to be ereected in the year of our Lord* 1783, *in honor of George Washington, the illustrious Commander-in-chief of the United States of America during the war which vindicated and secured their liberty, sovereignty, and independence.*'

"*Resolved, That a statue conformable to the above plan be executed by the best artist in Europe under the superintendance of the minister of the United States at the court of Versailles, and that money to defray the expense of the same be furnished from the treasury of the United States.*

"*Resolved, That the Secretary of Congress transmit to the minister at the court of Versailles the best resemblance of General Washington that can be procured for the purpose of having the above statue erected, together with the fittest description of the events which are to be the subject of the basso relievo.*"

Whether from a want of funds in the treasury or what, the minister to France never ordered the statue. The Commissioners who laid out he Federal City, set apart a place for it; but funds to build it were ›ver appropriated until 1852, and the original site had then been set ›art to the National Monument.

In 1799 Congress passed resolutions authorizing President Adams to correspond with Mrs. Washington, and ask her consent to the interment of the remains of her illustrious husband, under a monument to be erected by the United States in the Capitol at the City of Washington. Mrs. Washington gave her assent in the following letter:

"Taught by the great example I have so long had before me never to oppose my private wishes to the public will, I must consent to the request of Congress which you have had the goodness to transmit to me; and, in doing this, I need not, I cannot, say what a sacrifice of individual feeling I make to a sense of public duty."

But the monument was not erected, and the remains, therefore, were not removed from Mount Vernon.

In 1800, after long discussion, a bill passed one house for the erection of a "mausoleum of American granite and marble in a pyramidal form, 100 feet square at the base and of a proportional height."

In 1816 the subject was revived in a report by Mr. Huger, of South Carolina, from a joint committee, for a public monument, and the removal of the remaims, but nothing was done. In February of the same year the Legislature of Virginia authorized Gov. Nicholas to apply to Judge Bushrod Washington, then proprietor of Mount Vernon, for leave to remove the remains of General and Mrs. Washington from Mount Vernon to Richmond, to be placed under the monument proposed to be erected to the honor of Washington at the capital of the State. Judge Washington declined, and, among other reasons, stated the following:

"But obligations more sacred than anything which concerns myself—obligations with which I cannot dispense—command me to retain the mortal remains of my venerated uncle in the family vault where they are deposited. *It is his own will, and that will is to me a law which I dare not disobey.* He has himself directed his body should be placed there, and I cannot separate it from those of his near relatives, by which it is surrounded."

On the 13th of February, 1832, the two Houses of Congress appointed a joint committee to make arrangements for celebrating the centennial birth-day of George Washington. The Hon. Henry Clay was appointed chairman on the part of the Senate, and Hon. Philemon Thomas on the part of the House. Chief Justice John Marshall was requested to deliver an oration on the occasion, but declined, principally on the ground that, in addition to the pressure of his official duties, he was physically unable to perform the task, his voice having become so weak as to be almost inaudible even in a room not unusually large.

A resolution was recommended by the committee proposing that application be made to the proprietors of Mount Vernon for the body of George Washington, to be removed and deposited in the Capitol, in conformity with the resolution of December, 1799. It was provided also that the presiding officers of the two Houses should prescribe the order of such ceremonies as they might deem suitable to the occasion of the interment of the body of George Washington in the Capitol, on the 22d of February, and that the two Houses should attend them.

Mr. Clay supported the resolution in his usual eloquent and impressive style, and referred to the fact that those entrusted with the execution of the Capitol had already provided a vault under the centre of the rotundo for the express purpose. He thought it proper time to carry out the unredeemed pledge of Congress.

Mr. Forsyth opposed the resolution on the ground of the expressed wish of General Washington, who required in his will that his remains should rest in the family vault.

Mr. Tazewell and Mr. Tyler also opposed the resolution, which was supported by Mr. Webster, Mr. Sprague, and Mr. Bibb.

The resolution was finally adopted by a vote of 29 yeas to 15 nays.

On the next day the House of Representatives adopted a joint resolution, in which the Senate concurred, for associating the remains of the consort of Washington with his own, in their disinterment at Mount Vernon and reinterment in their appropriate mausoleum, the Capitol of the Union.

The Legislature of Virginia forthwith took action, at the suggestion of Governor Floyd, and on the 20th of February, 1832, passed the following resolutions.

"*Resolved unanimouly,* That the proprietors be earnestly requested, in the name of the people of this State, not to consent to the removal of the remains of General Washington from Mount Vernon."

And so intent was Governor Floyd on this head, that he appointed Judges Brooke and Marshall, and Major James Gibbon to be the bearers of the communication to Congress.

Application having been made to the proprietor, Mr. John A. Washington, he declined, on the ground that the will of Washington, in regard to his remains, had been recently carried into effect, and that they now repose in perfect tranquility, surrounded by those of other endeared members of the family.

Mr. Custis, the grandson of Mrs. Washington, gave his assent, and congratulated the Government upon the approaching consummation of a great act of national gratitude.

But no further steps were taken in regard to the removal, and, on the motion of Mr. Thomas, the correspondence was placed upon the journal, in order that it might be understood that Congress had gone to the extent of its power in the case.

The language of Washington's will on this subject, is as follows:

"The family vault at Mount Vernon requiring repairs, and being improperly situated besides, I desire that a new one, of Brick, and on a large scale, may be built at the foot of what is commonly called the Vineyard inclosure, on the ground which was marked out; in which my remains and those of my deceased relatives (now in the old vault,) and such others of my family as may choose to be entombed there, may be deposited. And it is my express desire that my corpse may be interred in a private manner, without parade or funeral oration."

As this does not expressly request that his remains should always be preserved in that vault, and as Mrs. Washington had not considered it any obstacle to a removal of her husband, it was thought that no objection would be made by the heirs.

There is certainly nothing improper in the repugnance manifested by Mr. John A. Washington to the removal of his uncle's remains, and many will be disposed to think that Congress erred in wishing to remove them; but the action of that body was based upon the idea that the Capitol of the nation was the most appropriate sepulchre for them, or, at all events, that they ought to be on ground common to the whole country, instead of being within the jurisdiction of any one State. Added to this was the consideration that the city which he founded and took so much interest in up to the day of his death, was a most appropriate place to receive his dust.

The action of the Virginia legislature was supposed to have been prompted in some measure by the desire to retain those sacred relics south of the Potomac, in the event of a dissolution of the Union, which the nullification excitement seemed to render possible.

But on all subsequent occasions, when a project for purchasing Mount Vernon or removing the remains has been mooted, they have taken action to prevent it. In a message of Governor Johnson to the Legislature of that State, after referring to the monument in process of erection in the Capitol square at Richmond, he makes the following recommendation:

"In connexion with this subject, I cannot refrain from respectfully but earnestly recommending to the Legislature the propriety of the purchase of Mount Vernon by the State of Virginia. And I do so at this time the more particularly, because there is reason to apprehend that it is about to pass into the hands of strangers. The importance of the acquisition of this property by the United States has frequently been brought to the attention of Congress, and it is surprising that this commendable project has met with so little favor. For this we should ever feel thankful, because if once the property of the Federal Government, we might never have been able to repurchase it. This should never be. Whilst we might reasonably prefer that it should be the property of the

Union rather than belong to any private individual, yet Virginia, and she only should be the owner and have control of this sacred and consecrated spot, where rest the mortal remains of her immortal son. Who else but Virginia should own this hallowed spot—to guard and protect the grave of him whose name will be revered as long as one shall live to admire American liberty? And should some ruthless hand ever disturb this sepulchre of the honored dead, or even change the primitive simplicity of his former residence, a sense of shame would come over every Virginian, and he would feel that that had been lost which could not be estimated in dollars and cents. If it can be purchased, then, upon fair and reasonable terms, let us do it at once, that we may preserve it in its primitive simplicity and beauty—to be freely resorted to by all admirers of true greatness and human liberty, and to be gazed on by all who may pass upon the beautiful Potomac.

"Considering the character of him whose name has thrown this halo of glory around the spot, and in view of the fact that (foremost as usual in whatever was good and great) he presided over the first Agricultural Society that ever met in Virginia, I do not know that the property could be more appropriately disposed of than to convert it into a model farm, and establish upon it a State Agricultural School. If this disposition should not meet your approbation, then it might be well to consider the propriety of establishing there a literary institution of some kind on a different basis. The first object, however, should be the acquisition of the property."

One cannot but wonder that Virginia did not invest the money in a purchase of Mount Vernon which she is now expending in a monument. As it is, she occupies the position of doing nothing herself, and preventing the nation from doing anything; for it seems to be agreed that it is the opposition of her representatives which prevents the purchase of the property by Congress.

Propositions for this purpose have been repeatedly introduced. One was to appropriate it for an army asylum; but as the army asylum will be admirably accommodated in the spacious marble edifice in course of erection in Washington county, there would seem to be no propriety in making a change; while there seems to be force in the following suggestion made by a writer in the Journal of Commerce some years since, if the fact stated be true:

"It is understood that there is a large sum in the Treasury, which has escheated to it in consequence of the decease, without heirs, of sailors and marines in the navy. The whole amount is estimated at three millions. There is a large sum due on account of prize money alone.

"The Government does not claim this fund, but merely the right of its safe keeping. There is no chance that it will ever be called for. It would be very proper, therefore, to appropriate the sum, or a portion of it, to the purchase of Mount Vernon, and the establishment there of an institution for the benefit of invalid and superannuated seamen and mariners. If the fund does not belong to them, it belongs to nobody. It would seem that they have, as a body, a right to all its benefits, at least to the benefit of the interest of the fund."

Another proposition, which is not perhaps inconsistent with the one just stated, is to make it the residence of the Vice President, in order that he may be on hand in case of accident to the President, the Government having been, at the time of President Harrison's death, without any head at the capital for the space of two days. Recently a committee of the Senate has reported in favor of purchasing it for an agricultural farm in connexion with the Patent Office.

In relation to these or any other plans which may be suggested for preserving and opening to the public an access to this now much-neglected spot, it can hardly be doubted that they would find favor throughout the country.

In 1832, Greenough's statue was ordered by Congress. It was intended to have been placed in the rotunda over the vault, but being found too large was removed to the Eastern park.

In 1853, immediately after the inauguration of Mills' statue of General Jackson, in Lafayette square, Congress passed, unanimously, a resolution appropriating $50,000 for an equestrian statue of Washington, upon which Mills is now engaged.

Thus much for the action of Congress on the subject of a monument to Washington. Other works of art have been executed by order of Congress, which may, perhaps, be properly classed among monumental structures—such are the exquisite figure of History and the Car of Time, in the Representatives Hall, the statues of Peace and War, and the figures upon the tympanum of the Eastern portico of the Capitol, the bust of Washington over the door leading from the rotunda, and the group of Columbus and the Indian Girl, by Persico, and of the Western Settler, by Greenough.*

It should be mentioned that in the long discussions which took place in 1799 and 1800, objection was made by some prominent members to the erection by Congress of any monument to an individual, however distinguished, on the ground that it was a bad precedent for the Government to engage in any such undertaking. "If we decline," said

---

* Concerning the position of these last statues, the following remarks, by Greenough, seem to be very appropriate:

"The position of the group of Columbus and the Indian girl is anomalous and absurd; anomalous, because it invades the front view of the portico, crowds the facade and hides another statue by the same artist; absurd, because it treats the building as somewhat on which to mount into conspicuous view, not as a noble and important vase which it is called humbly to adorn and illustrate. * * * The railings which have been placed around the statues of the Capitol accuse a want of respect for the public property. They accuse it, without remedying it; for, in spite of their protection, perhaps because of it, the statues of Columbus and of Washington have received more injury in the few years that they have been so guarded, than many figures wrought before the birth of Christ have suffered in coming to us through the so-called dark ages."—*Æsthetics in Washington, page* 72.

Mr. Macon, "to rear one to Washington, no one who succeeds him can expect one reared to his memory. On the other hand, if we erect one, every pretender to greatness will aim at the same distinction." Reference was made to the abuses which had grown out of the system in Europe, and the ground was taken that they should be the results of individual effort—voluntary contributions. But the sentiment of the country has been rather favorable to such structures. Not only has Congress erected two statues; but in almost every State more or less action has been taken on the subject.

The Legislatures of Virginia and North Carolina have erected statues in their State houses. The first is by Houdon, a good likeness, in the costume of commander-in-chief, which has been objected to by critiques as not sufficiently graceful and classical; the second by Canova, in a sitting posture with the Roman costume. There is one at the State house, at Boston, by Chantry; the costume is a military cloak, which displays the figure to advantage. Neither of the two last are good likenesses, the artists having embodied their ideas of Washington's character, rather than attempted any resemblance. The statue by Greenough, before referred to, is in a sitting posture, and is admirably executed. The likeness is perfect; the costume Roman, which, whatever the classical scholar may say, does not suit the taste of a majority of those who see it. Virginia is about expending $100,000 on a monument at Richmond; Maryland has reared one at Baltimore, a noble column; the Bunker hill monument, the Battle monument at Baltimore, those at Concord and Lexington, and the equestrian statue of Jackson, also a bronze statue of De Witt Clinton, at Greenwood cemetery, were mostly erected by voluntary contributions.

In New York and Philadelphia various projects have been started; and in the former, the whole population once turned out, marched up to Hamilton square, laid a corner stone, and then marched down again; but the stone has ever since remained alone in its glory. It is understood that a few wealthy citizens have recently subscribed for a statue by Powers. The difficulty has generally been, that the plans were on so extravagant a scale that no subscriber could ever hope to see it completed. Amidst all the local projects there has always been a call for something like a National Monument, on a scale worthy of the nation—"a monument," in the language of Mr. Winthrop, "that shall bespeak the gratitude, not of the State, or of Cities, or of Governments, not of separate communities, or of official bodies; but of the people, the whole people of the nation: a national monument erected by the citizens of the United States of America."

On the 26th September, 1833, a number of citizens of Washington assembled together, and on that and several subsequent meetings digested a plan for erecting a National Monument.

It was confidently believed that, after such a grand mausoleum was completed by the contributions of the whole people, no State or individual would object to a removal of the remains.

Whether this should be accomplished or not, it would be a kind of rallying point for patriotism, and a noble emblem of attachment to the Union and its founders.

Among those who first officiated were Daniel Brent, William Brent, Joseph Gales, sr., James Kearney, Joseph Gales, jr., Peter Force, W. W. Seaton, John McLelland, Pishey Thompson, Thomas Carberry, George Watterston, and William Cranch, the present venerable chief justice of the circuit court of the District of Columbia, who was the first vice president. Chief Justice Marshall was chosen as president, and accepted in the following letter:

RICHMOND, *November 25th*, 1833.

"I received yesterday your letter of the 22nd, informing me that the Washington Monument Society has done me the honor to choose me as its president. You are right in supposing that the most ardent wish of my heart is to see some lasting testimonial of the grateful affection of his country erected to the memory of her first citizen. I have always wished it, and have always thought that the Metropolis of the Union was the fit place for this National Monument. I cannot therefore refuse to take any place which the society may assign to me, and though my advanced age forbids the hope of being useful, I am encouraged by the name of the first vice president to believe that in him ample conversation will be found for any defect in the president."

After Judge Marshall's death Mr. Madison became the president, and since his death, the successive presidents of the United States have held that position. Many of the most distinguished public men of the country have been and still are connected with it; and it speaks well for the character of the gentlemen who have had the immediate management, that not a whisper has ever been breathed against them of want of good faith, or other than scrupulous and economical application of the funds to the object, while not one of them has ever directly or indirectly received any compensation.

Seldom have the weekly meetings of the board failed for want of a quorum. We mention these facts because such assiduity and fidelity in attending to the duties of a volunteer association are not common, and in order to prevent this society and its collections from being confounded with others for the State monuments, where collections were made at nearly the same time, and where it is alleged that the funds have been wasted.

How to raise the funds was of course the first question; and a subscription of not exceeding one dollar from every citizen of the United States was finally proposed, under the belief that no one of moderate means would refuse so small a contribution, while none would be deterred from giving, because not able to put down as much as his neighbor. It was confidently believed that several hundred thousand dollars would be received. But the dollar limitation was found to be an embarrassment, chiefly it is presumed, because collectors found it required more labor and time than the commission would compensate for. And then people distrusted and could not believe that such small sums would ever be accounted for. The fact that the great fire in New York and the revulsion of money affairs occurred about this time, interfered also very materially with the collection. Twenty-eight thousand dollars was the whole amount received. This sum was invested in stock, and the interest regularly re-invested, and, in this way the sum had increased to $40,000, when the monument was commenced in 1848; but active operations in the way of collections ceased for a number of years.

At length about the year 1846, a new subscription was opened; but without any restriction as to amount. Great difficulty was and still is experienced in obtaining the right kind of agents, men who were well known, possessed the public confidence, of good education and agreeable address, with some knowledge of human nature. If such can be procured who have real heart for the work they are very apt to be exceedingly sensitive and easily discouraged at rebuffs. It is unpleasant to ask for money and most men prefer to engage in any other pursuits.

It has been remarked that in the collections for the National Monument the largest sums have generally been collected in those districts where, from the sparsity of the population and the absence of any great resources for wealth, the least was to have been expected. Thus, an agent in the mountainous districts of Virginia, who had to travel two or three miles from one house to another, sent to Washington more money than the agent at the flourishing city of Richmond. Large collections have been made in the retired parts of Georgia and Florida.*

---

* A statement, in detail, of the collections is, we understand, to be published hereafter in the papers, and corrected every six months. Up to May, 1854, the collection district which had contributed the largest amount, in proportion to population, was Fayette county, Pennsylvania, where the amount was over $2,200.

In Washington city there had been collected upwards of $12,000, with a number of annual subscribers. This does not include the amounts received at

One reason for this undoubtedly is, that the people of the country are less frequently called upon for all manner of objects than those of cities; but there can be no question that there is more poetry and sentiment in rural districts. They have fewer books and distractions, and consequently read over the history of their country more frequently. In the long winter nights they hear the "old folks" talk about old times, and occasionally they come across a revolutionary pensioner, who fights his battles over again.

The whole amount collected up to the 1st May 1854, was $231,000, and the receipts have averaged about $2,000 a month.

The most constant efforts however are required to keep the receipts up to the line of the expenditures. Notwithstanding the number of agents who have been employed, it is doubtful whether one-fifth of the population have been applied to. Masonic and Odd-Fellows Associations have given largely, Washington having been a member of the former fraternity. Two or three cities have contributed by their municipal authorities in money,* and it is confidently expected that every city in the Union will furnish its quota.

Every State in the Union, and a large number of cities, towns and associations have contributed blocks with suitable devices. Some of these are very large and costly, with the finest basso relievos upon them. Michigan sends a block of native copper, with letters of native silver, while an immense variety of beautiful marbles and granites are represented in the others; indeed the display here made has suggested the idea, which it is hoped will be carried out, of completing the interior finish of the capitol extension, with specimens of every kind of American material. The Swiss Confederation sent a block from the Alps, and almost every week some new one arrives. All these add greatly to the interest with which the monument is regarded, and we cannot but believe that the work will continue slowly but steadily to progress.

It became necessary at an early day to decide upon a plan, lithographic designs of which furnished to contributors, with receipts appended, would, it was thought, aid the collectors in their operations, and, from a large number of designs, which were submitted, that of Robert Mills was finally selected, consisting of an obelisk of great

---

Monument Place, the Patent Office, and from the city government, which amounts to as much more. New York, Brooklyn, and Albany, a little less than $4,700; St. Louis, about $2,500; Cincinnati, $2,900. California has sent more than any other State in proportion to population. Considerable sums have been received at the polls, and in taking the census. Better collections have been made at the South than at the North.

* Washington, $2,500; Georgetown, D. C., $100; Lafayette, Louisiana, $500; Savannah, Georgia, $100 a year until completed.

height, surrounded by a colonade of doric columns, called a pantheon, to contain revolutionary relics, statues, &c.

This is so much a mere matter of taste that it is not easy to say what design would have best suited the public at large, and satisfied, to a reasonable degree, the critics, in architecture. On the one hand, the union of the Egyptian obelisk with the Grecian pantheon is considered by artists a great violation of proprieties. But for the satisfaction of such be it known, that there is no probability that the pantheon will ever be built, the obelisk alone being about as much as the Society can hope to receive the funds for. The cost of the obelisk, which is first to be completed, is estimated at $552,000; and that of the obelisk and pantheon, forming the entire monument, at $1,122,000. Should the whole amount be subscribed, and a structure at the base be added, it can be altered so as to conform more nearly to the obelisk. At least such a change might be made that the base of the obelisk will be visible, so that it may not seem, as now, to stand on columns. On the other hand, the agents say that the design is very generally admired by those who are called upon for subscriptions, except in some of the more critical classes in northern cities. To such an extent are our ideas of beauty formed by education! And do we not sometimes make up our judgment rather by arbitrary rules as to harmony laid down in books than by any real want of harmony between two orders of architecture? For our own part we should have thought that something might have been designed more peculiarly expressive of its object and more American in its details, less of a mere imitation of the ancients, something which would have embodied in it the trees and products peculiar to our country. Nothing attracts more admiration in the Capitol than what is sometimes called the American order of architecture, columns formed of bundles of corn-stalks, with capitals of corn, and the columns of the circle between the rotunda and Senate chamber with capitals of tobacco leaves. But our artists and architects have not heretofore shown much originality or taste in devising monuments on a large scale, whatever may be said of smaller works in cemeteries. Some years ago the committee for erecting a monument at Hamilton Square, in New York, advertised for plans, and some forty or fifty designs were sent in and exhibited at the Art Union. A more grotesque and absurd looking group of light-houses, pyramids, and nondescript looking structures never were got together. Only one, that of Frazee, received the faintest modicum of praise, and that, if we recollect right, was a superb copy of the Parthenon, to cost about five millions of dollars! After this exhibition of what a number of artists could offer, we became reconciled to the design of the National Monument, which, either as a whole or as a simple obelisk, was far superior in every respect to anything here presented. To be sure it would have been desirable to have something a little less like a second edition of Bunker Hill Monument, and which could present internal as well as outward attractions. The stones presented by States and associations are to line the inside walls at each landing of the staircase, and must be viewed by artificial light—a great disadvantage. These were not, however, thought of until after the work had progressed for some time. *And it is remarkable that long as the plan was before the public, and when there was yet an opportunity for change, not a word was said by those who are now so ready to find fault.*

But it is too late now to make any material changes in the obelisk, which, with all the objections to it, presents some decided advantages.

First. It is of all monuments the strongest and most enduring, next to that of the pyramid. In 1800, when the question in Congress was between adopting the statue of '83, or a mausoleum, in pyramidal form, it was stated in debate that, without any concert whatever, a remarkable concurrence had taken place between West, Trumbull, and other respectable artists, who gave an unequivocal preference to a mausoleum. A mausoleum would last for ages, and would present the same imperishable appearance two thousand years hence that it would now; whereas a statue would only remain until some civil convulsion or foreign invasion or flagitious conqueror, or lawless mob, should dash it into atoms, or until some invading barbarian should transport it as a trophy of his guilt to a foreign shore. Besides a statue was minute, trivial, perishable. It was a monument erected to all that crowd of estimable but subordinate personages that soar in a region elevated indeed above common characters, but which was infinitely below that of Washington.

Secondly. It is like the government and character of Washington, simple and majestic, with no attempt at ornament. It cannot well be spoiled in building, or by bad sculpture. We could not hope to rival the magnificent productions of the Old World in sculpture, however creditable the works of our artists may have been in one or two instances.

Thirdly. It will excel all others in one respect, that of height, as will be seen by the following comparison between this and some of the most celebrated monuments and churches:

No.		Height—feet.
1.	St. Antoine's Column, at Rome	135
2.	Capitol, at Washington	140

No.		Height—feet
3.	Principal Tower of Smithsonian Institution	145
4.	Trajan's Column, at Rome	145
5.	Napoleon's Column, at Paris	150
6.	Washington's Column, at Baltimore	180
7.	The Great Obelisk, Thebes	200
8.	Bunker Hill Monument, Boston	220
9.	Column of Delhi	262
10.	Trinity Church, New York	264
11.	St. Paul's Cathedral, (Dome,) London	320
12.	St. Peter's Cathedral, (Dome,) Rome	465
13.	Tower of the Cathedral of Strasbourg	460
14.	Great Pyramid of Egypt	480
15.	Tower of Malines	350
16.	Washington National Monument, at Dist. of Col	517½

The foundation of the obelisk is laid 81 feet square, 8 feet below the ground, and is contracted so as to be 61 feet 10 inches square at the top, an elevation of 25 feet of solid masonry.

The obelisk is commenced at the height of 17½ feet above the ground, 55 feet square, cased with marble, with walls 15 feet thick, leaving a cavity of 25 feet. It will be ascended by stairs in the inside, and by machinery, to an elevation of 517½ feet.* Something of a climb this! To ascend by zigzag staircases a thousand steps, and view the presentation blocks as you go along, will be a good day's work. The workmen go up and down now by machinery. But, if Washington's sarcophagus should ever be placed in the centre, there would seem to be a kind of sacrilege in riding up above it. The only opening, besides the doors, will be a large star, near the top on each side. It has been proposed to cap it with one large glass cone. The obelisk will stand on a platform or pedestal extending on every side, and having arched rooms well lighted from above, in which may be deposited the reliques of Washington now preserved at the Patent Office.

As to the material, the outside is constructed of what is known as Symington's large crystal marble, procured from the vicinity of Baltimore. The main body of the wall is of blue gneiss, and with this the interior is lined, except where blocks presented by States or associations have been inserted. The quality of the material and its

* The visitor will find it difficult, from the present appearance of the work, to realize how it will look when completed. Standing alone, and not contrasting with buildings around, with no windows to break the wall, it looks low, although over 150 feet high from the ground; and it is only by pacing around, that one perceives that it covers more space than one of the largest sized double houses, such as have a hall in the centre with rooms on each side.

capacity to sustain pressure and resist frost were most satisfactorily tested in some experiments made at two different times, under the direction of the Department of the Interior.*

"Mr. Robert Mills, the architect thus reports, in June 26, 1849, the result of the experiments to determine the strength of the marble proposed for the facing of the walls of the Patent Office wing buildings, obtained from the same quarries that supply the marble used for the outer casing or facing of the monument, as determined by Professor Page and himself, and with the aid of a powerful hydrostatic press, (Bramah principle,) constructed by the Superintendent of Machinery at the Navy Yard, Mr. Ellis. We had supplied ourselves with eight marble blocks, or cubes of two inches square, taken from several points, promiscuously, in the quarries.

The specific gravity of this marble had been previously ascertained by Dr. Page, when he reported on the durability of certain stones submitted to him by the Regents of the Smithsonian Institution, namely, 2857.

Cube No. 1, subjected to the press, bore (10,000) ten thousand pounds, before exhibiting any fracture, and was crushed under the pressure of (11,000) eleven thousand pounds.

No. 2 was crushed under the force of ten thousand six hundred (10,600) pounds; No. 3, 11,800 lbs.; No. 4, 10,825 lbs.; No. 5, 9,750 lbs.; No. 6, about the same; No. 7, 11,375 lbs.; and No. 8, 10,500 lbs.

The average of all these exceeds ten thousands pounds, which equals in strength the granites.

The atmospheric action on the same description of marble, was ascertained by Dr. Page to be the fifteenth part of one grain, (the specimens were cut into inch cubes, and the time of action four weeks,) compared with the large crystal marble of New York, (like that used in the facing of the General Post Office,) it was found to be a moiety. Port Deposite granite lost ninety-one hundredths of a grain, and Trinity Church five grains, and light colored sand stone 1 58-100 grains, while the Patent Office light sandstone 18 60-100 grains.

The practical application of these experiments to the work in marble at the Washington National Monument, may be now presented under the following formula:

1st. Given the height of the monument 500 feet, what is the weight of a cubical column of marble twelve inches square at the base.

The weight of a cubic foot of this marble, 180 lbs.; by 500 feet=90,000 lbs.; which is the pressure upon one square foot at the base of this column.

2d. Given a cube of two inches, or a base of four square inches, which, by experiment will bear a pressure of ten thousand lbs.; to determine what a square foot of marble at the base of the monument would bear before crushing.

Then if a base of marble of 4 square inches will bear a pressure of 10,000 lbs.; what will a base of marble of 144 square inches bear?

As 4 in.: 10,000 lbs : : 144 into 360,000 lbs., or four times the actual weight

* A discoloration which appears in the marble in the monument, and which has been attributed to the presence of iron, is, we are informed, caused by the strips of lead which are placed between the blocks along with the cement, and undergo at first a partial decomposition until the cement becomes hard. It may, we are told, be washed off.

of a column of marble 500 feet high, pressing on a square foot at the base of the monument.

We subjected also a block of the *Blue Stone* (gneiss) of the Potomac, which forms the foundation and backing to the marble of the structure, to the test of pressure, and found that a block squaring but 3.37½ square inches bore a pressure of 13,375 lbs. before fracture.

The above calculations are all based upon a *perpendicular* pressure. The form of that part of the Monument now erecting being the obelisk, the face or wall continually diminishes as it rises, from a square of 55 feet at the base to a square of 35 feet at the apex, consequently the centre of gravity is continually changing, each block of marble forming the face actually having to bear scarcely a third of the superincumbent weight.

A word on the strength of foreign marble, &c. Statuary marble of Italy bore under the same square of base 12,625 lbs.; the granite of Normandy 10,512 lbs.; the granite of the east 13,000 lbs.; and porphry 39,000. The New York marble of the kind facing the General Post Office building stood a pressure of 15,625 lbs.

In answer to an inquiry in relation to the cause of the spauling or scaling off of the edges of the marble near the base of the monument, the superintendent states that the lead used between the joints the first season was rather light, the consequence was that the joints were close, and the weight above pressing down forced the mortar out, after becoming hard, and carried the edge of the marble with it. After the first season the thickness of the lead was increased, since which time nothing of the kind has occurred, neither has any further spauling taken place for the last four years, although 120 feet has been added to the weight which was on the monument at the time the spauling took place. He also states that the same thing took place at the Girard College in Philadelphia, so much so, that they were obliged to saw out the joints.

The site upon which the monument is being erected, was set apart by the President of the United States and the Board of Managers, under an act of Congress of January 21, 1848, embraces upwards of thirty acres, near the Potomac river, directly west of the Capitol, and south of the executive mansion, on the ground selected by the United States Commissioners, when they laid out the city, as the position for the statue of Washington, heretofore referred to as having been voted by the Continental Congress in 1783. It is so marked on the plan submitted by them to Congress in 1793, during the Presidency of Washington.

This fact is sufficient. *Washington himself died in the belief that on this spot he would be commemorated.*

But the position is an admirable one, in other respects. Although, from some parts of the city the ground appears low, yet, on visiting the spot, one cannot but be struck with the commanding view presented of the river and all the public buildings. It is at the intersection of two great avenues, Louisiana, running from the City Hall, and Virginia, from the Navy Yard, while the ground or mall from the Capitol, by the

Smithsonian Institute to the monument, and thence to the President's house, is being handsomely laid off into public gardens from designs by Downing.

Immediately east of the Monument Square is a beautiful site for the equestrian statue now being modelled by Clarke Mills.

We cannot better close this article than by quoting the concluding words of Mr. Winthrop's admirable address on laying the corner stone, an event which took place on the 4th July, 1848.

"Let the column which we are about to construct, be at once a pledge and an emblem of perpetual union! Let the foundations be laid, let the superstructure be built up and cemented, let each stone be raised and riveted, in a spirit of national brotherhood! And may the earliest ray of the rising sun—till that sun shall set to rise no more—draw forth from it daily, as from the fabled statue of antiquity, a strain of national harmony, which shall strike a responsive cord in every heart throughout the Republic!

"Proceed, then, fellow-citizens, with the work for which you have assembled! Lay the corner-stone of a monument which shall adequately bespeak the gratitude of the whole American People to the illustrious Father of his Country! Build it to the skies; you cannot outreach the loftiness of his principles! Found it upon the massive and eternal rock: you cannot make it more enduring than his fame! Construct it of the peerless Parian marble: you cannot make it purer than his life! Exhaust upon it the rules and principles of ancient and modern art: you cannot make it more proportionate than his character!"

CHAPTER V.

THE SMITHSONIAN INSTITUTION.

SINGULARITY OF THE BEQUEST—WHO WAS SMITHSON?—DISCUSSIONS ON PROPRIETY OF ACCEPTING THE BEQUEST—RECEPTION AND INVESTMENT OF THE FUNDS—PLANS PROPOSED BY ADAMS, WAYLAND, RUSH, ROBBINS, TAPPAN, CHOATE, OWEN, AND MARSH—CHARTER—DISCUSSION AMONG THE REGENTS, AND THEIR RESULT—VIEWS OF SECRETARY HENRY—ADDITIONAL BEQUEST—BUILDING.

"To the United States of America, to found at Washington, under the name of the Smithsonian Institution, an establishment for the increase and diffusion of knowledge among men." Such was the language by which, in a will, made in 1826, James Smithson disposed of the whole of his property, amounting to something more than half a million of dollars. It was, in every point of view, a remarkable bequest. Such a donation from a citizen of Europe, would be remarkable under any circumstances; but it is much more singular coming from an Englishman, endued with no small degree of pride of country and lineage, if we may judge from the pains he takes, in the caption of his will, to detail his descent from the nobility. He is not known to have ever visited the United States, or to have had any friend residing here. Mr. Rush informs us that "he was a natural son of the Duke of Northumberland, his mother being Mrs. Macie, of an ancient family in Wiltshire of the name of Hungerford—he was educated at Oxford, where he took an honorary degree in 1786; he took the name of James Lewis Macie until a few years after he left the University, when he changed it to Smithson. He does not appear to have had any fixed home, living in lodgings when in London, and occasionally, a year or two at a time, in the cities on the continent, as Paris, Berlin, Florence, and Genoa, at which last place he died. The ample provision made for him by the Duke of Northumberland, with retired and simple habits, enabled him to accumulate the fortune which passed to the United States. He interested himself little in questions of government, being devoted to science, and chiefly to chemistry. This had introduced him to the society of Cavendish Wollaston and others, advantageously known to the Royal Society in London, of which he was a member."

In a paper relative to one of the publications of the Smithsonian Institution, read before a scientific society at Dublin, it is stated, on the authority of Chambers' Journal, that he had gained a name by the analysis of minute quantities, and that "it was he who caught a tear as it fell from a lady's cheek, and detected the salts and other substances which it held in solution." In a notice of his scientific pursuits, by Professor Johnson, of Philadelphia, there are enumerated twenty-four papers or treatises by Smithson, published in the Transactions of the Royal Society, and other scientific journals of the day, containing articles on mineralogy, geology, and more especially mineral chemistry. In the Annals of Philosophy (vol. 22, page 30) he has a brief tract on the method of making coffee. The small case of his personal effects, which is to be preserved in a separate apartment of the Institution, consists chiefly of minerals and chemical apparatus.*

The will indicates a degree of sensitiveness on the subject of his illegitimacy. He starts with a declaration of pedigree. "I, James Smith-

* It is to be hoped that the Institution will publish in a convenient form all such particulars as can be obtained concerning its founder; also all his writings, and the discussions on receiving the bequest and establishing the Institution. Indeed it is remarkable that this has not been done before. The silver ware, among his personal effects, should be cleansed up and kept in good order.

son, son of Hugh, first Duke of Northumberland, and Elizabeth, heiress of the Hungerfords of Audley, and niece of Charles the proud, Duke of Somerset, now residing in Bentinck street, Cavendish square, do make this my last will and testament."

Nothing but an apprehension that some imputation might be cast upon his birth, would have led him thus to proclaim that some of the best blood of England flowed in his veins. Having thus demonstrated that he had no occasion to be ashamed of his descent, he goes on as if to show his contempt for the distinctions made by the law in such cases, and gives the whole income of his property to a nephew, Henry James Hungerford, heretofore called Henry James Dickinson, for life, and, after his death the property to the child or children, *legitimate or illegitimate*, of said nephew. But should the nephew marry, he empowers him to make a jointure. On the death of this nephew without issue, the bequest to the United States to take effect.

It has been inferred by some that he must have dictated this will while suffering under some slight or mortification in consequence of his birth, when, in a feeling of disgust he determined to bestow his liberality elsewhere; and so brief an expression does look a little like a mere whim or caprice of the moment, although made long before his death. Chambers' Journal mentions that he had at one time bequeathed his property to the Royal Society, but changed the disposition of it in consequence of some offence taken at the action of that Institution. It is a pity that the cause of offence is not given, since it might possibly have thrown some light upon the kind of Institution he had in view; but it is hardly reasonable to suppose that it had any connection with his paternity. The probability is, that he saw in the United States a comparatively unoccupied field, where such an Institution would exert more influence and be better known than among the crowd of well-endowed establishments in the old world.

The bequest was announced to Congress by President Jackson in a message on the 17th December, 1835. In each House a report was made on the subject. In the Senate, on the 5th January, 1836, Mr. Leigh, from the Judiciary Committee, reported a resolution to authorize the appointment of an agent to take the necessary proceedings in the English Court of Chancery for the recovery of the same.

The points considered by the committee were whether it was competent for the United States, whether it comported with their dignity, whether, all circumstances considered, it was expedient and proper that they should appear as suitors in the courts of justice in England, to assert their claim to the legacy, as trustees for the intended charitable institution to be founded at Washington. The committee thought that, whatever doubts might exist as to whether Government could appropriate any part of their revenue collected from the nation at large for the endowment of a literary or charitable institution in the District, no such question was involved here, as the Government is to accept as trustee and parens-patriæ of the District, in which capacity, and as the only Legislature of the District, they might properly appropriate funds to pay the expense of procuring the legacy.*

On the 19th January, Mr. J. Q. Adams reported from a select committee to the House of Representatives a law providing for the same object as Mr. Leigh's resolution, and accompanied it by a report,† in which he gives the following more detailed account of Smithson's descent, which adds to the singularity of this bequest, inasmuch as it shows that a brother of the testator fought against us in the Revolution:

"Nearly two centuries since, in 1660, the ancestor of his own name, Hugh Smithson, immediately after the restoration of the Royal family of the Stuarts, received from Charles the Second, as a reward for his eminent services to that house during the civil wars, the dignity of Baronet of England—a dignity still held by the Dukes of Northumberland as descendents from the same Hugh Smithson. The father of the testator, by his marriage with the Lady Elizabeth Seymour, who was descended by a female line from the ancient Percies, and by the subsequent creation of George the Third in 1766, became the first Duke of Northumberland. His son and successor, the brother of the testator, known in the history of our Revolutionary war by the name of Lord Percy, was present, as a British officer, at the sanguinary opening scene of our Revolutionary war at Lexington, and at the battle of Bunker Hill; and was the bearer to the British Government of the despatches from the commander-in-chief of the Royal forces announcing the event of that memorable day."

Further on the venerable reporter proceeds as follows:

"The father of the testator, upon forming his alliance with the heiress of the family of the Percies, assumed by an act of the British Parliament that name, and under it became Duke of Northumberland. But, renowned as is the name of Percy in the historical annals of England; resounding as it does from the summit of the Cheviot Hills to the ears of our children, in the ballad of Chevy Chase, with the classical commentary of Addison; freshened and renovated in our memory as it has recently been, from the purest fountain of poetical inspiration, in the loftier strain of Alnwick castle, tuned by a bard of our own native land,

* Senate Doc. 42, 24th Congress, 1st session.

† H. R. Doc. 181, 24th Congress, 1st session.

(Fitz Greene Halleck;) doubly immortalized as it is in the deathless dramas of Shakespeare; 'confident against the world in arms,' as it may have been in ages long past, and may still be in the virtues of its present possessors by inheritance, *let the trust of James Smithson to the United States of America be faithfully executed by their Representatives in Congress*—let the result accomplish his object, 'the increase and diffusion of knowledge among men,' and a wreath of more unfading virtue shall entwine itself in the lapse of future ages around the name of Smithson than the united hands of tradition, history, and poetry have braided around the name of Percy, through the long perspective in ages past of a thousand years."

This eloquent passage in Mr. Adams' report was adverted to by Mr. Preston, in the Senate, when the report of Mr. Leigh was taken up for consideration,* and he said there was danger, that in view of this subject, the imagination should be led away by Chevy Chase ballads; and he, with Mr. Calhoun, contended that Congress had not the power, under the Constitution, to receive it, (a power which Mr. Adams had taken for granted.) His argument was that they had no right to establish a national university, and if they could not do that directly, they could not do it indirectly by acting as trustee for others. He thought the donation had been partly made with a view to immortalize the donor, and that it was too cheap a way of conferring immortality. He had no idea of the District of Columbia being used as a fulcrum to raise foreigners to immortality, by getting Congress, as parens-patriæ of the District, to accept donations. Besides, in this instance it could not be said to be for the especial benefit of the District—that was only the location—whatever benefit Washington City derived, would be but incidental from the buildings being there. As well might it be said that the Patent Office and other establishments of Government were for the especial benefit of the District, although advantages were derived therefrom. The bequest was for the benefit of the whole of mankind, and he thought there was no power under the Constitution to legislate for the education or exercise of philanthropy to the whole world—that was reserved to the States. If they accepted this donation every whipper-snapper that had been traducing our country might think proper to have his name distinguished in the same way. It was not consistent with the dignity of the country, to accept even the grant of a man of noble birth and lineage. In opposition to this view, Messrs. Clayton and Southard contended for the right to establish a national university, and Messrs. Buchanan, Walker, Davis and others, thought that

* See Congressional Globe, May 2d, 1836, for this debate, which is quite interesting; we do not profess to give the words of the speakers, but the substance.

question had no bearing on the subject; but all of them favored the present bill. Congress had established other literary institutions in the District, and, though the policy of doing so had been questioned, no objection had ever been made as to the constitutional right. It could not be doubted that the States might establish such institutions in their midst, and, by the acts of cession, Maryland and Virginia, had vested all their power in Congress. There was no question but that Smithson, in his lifetime, had a right to establish a college at Washington, and call it a National or a Smithsonian University, and Congress by accepting would only act as the trustee of the City of Washington, to whose benefit it would ensue, even if not made expressly therefor. The institutions already established here, were mainly for the benefit of Washington, although students from other places would also be benefitted thereby. So the Smithsonian, while intended for the benefit of all mankind, would make itself chiefly felt in Washington. The act accepting the bequest, was finally passed by yeas 31, nays 7, and it became a law on the 1st July, 1836. Under it Mr. Richard Rush was appointed agent, who, on the 12th May, 1838, announced to the Secretary of State, that the court of chancery had decided in favor of the United States, after hearing all parties interested, and also the Attorney General, in behalf of the Queen, (who interposed however no objections to the final disposition of the fund,) and with a despatch which was attributed in part to the fact, that it was the first time this Government had ever been a party to a suit in England.

The whole amount received, in September, 1838, was $508,318 46, the most of which was immediately invested in Arkansas State bonds, by the Secretary of the Treasury, and not one dollar of principal or interest has that State ever paid, nor do we know that any effort has ever been made by the Legislature or the people to wipe off this stain. This fact has no particular bearing on our subject; because, Congress having pledged the faith of the United States, made good the deficiency in the fund out of the treasury, but it cannot be too often adverted to, for the constant mention of it may some day raise the sense of shame to as great a pitch among the citizens of the State thus disgraced, as it has already done upon the cheek of every citizen who has any pride of country.

The President, through the Secretary of State, invited gentlemen of learning and distinction to submit their views as to the best method of applying the Smithsonian bequest, and very full replies were received from Mr. J. Q. Adams, President Wayland, Mr. Richard Rush, and Presidents Cooper and Chapin.*

* House of Reps. 25th Congress, 1838, Doc. No. 11.

The first suggested that annual courses of lectures on the principal sciences, physical and mathematical, moral, political, and literary, to be delivered, not by permanent professors, but by persons annually appointed, with a liberal compensation for each course, were among the means well adapted to the end of increasing and diffusing knowledge *among men.*

He subsequently embodied his views much more at length in a somewhat famous report, made to Congress in 1839,* the leading idea embodied in which was a great Observatory and a Nautical Almanac, to which the whole income was to be devoted for seven years, which, he thought, would be long enough to completely establish and endow it, then another department was to be taken up, such as a Botanic Garden; next a Museum of Natural History, or a Library, and so on through all the objects which tend to the increase of knowledge, each of which was to be made complete, before commencing a new one. The Observatory feature he abandoned on the erection of one by the Government. Every one will unite with him in that part of his letter where he expresses his anxiety to "guard against the canker of almost all charitable foundations—jobbing for parasites and sops for hungry incapacity." For the economical management of the fund, and the periodical application of it to appropriate expenditures, he recommends that it be invested in a board of trustees, to consist partly of members of Congress, with the Secretaries of the Departments, the Attorney General, the Mayor of the city of Washington, and one or more inhabitants of the District of Columbia, to be incorporated as trustees of the Smithsonian fund, with a secretary and treasurer in one person, and to be the only salaried person of the board; to be appointed for four years, and be capable of reappointment, but removable for adequate cause by a majority of the board." These suggestions were, to some extent, adopted in the provisions of the act which provides for the Board of Regents, also a suggestion made by Mr. Rush, that the affairs should be subject to the investigation of the President, aided by a standing board, to consist of the chief officers of the Government. And for the good government of the Institution, the standing board to call in the assistance of three or more scientific or literary persons unconnected with it.

President Wayland recommended a "National University," occupying the space between the close of a collegiate education and a professional school; that there should be public lectures on Latin, Greek, Hebrew, and the Oriental languages; that all the modern languages of any use to the scholar should be taught; astronomy, engineering, civil

* House Reps. 27th Congress, 1839, 2d Sess., Doc. No. 857. Also Doc. 277 1840, 1st session, 26th Congress.—*Congressional Globe, April* 12, 1842.

and military; the art of war, beginning where it is left off at West Point; chemistry, geology, mining, music, and poetry; political economy, intellectual philosophy, physiology, vegetable and animal; anatomy, human, comparative; history, the laws of nations and the general principles of law, the Constitution of the United States.

Mr. Senator Robbins, of Rhode Island, on occasion of moving for a joint committee on the subject on the 10th January, 1839, advocated something similar to this of President Wayland, in a very elegant and classical speech. He proposed for the present to make the Smithsonian an independent institution; but cherished the hope that it might hereafter form one of a number of colleges to constitute a university, to be established in Washington, and endowed in a manner worthy of the nation. The joint committee was appointed, Mr. Adams being chairman of that on the part of the House, but the committee being unable to agree, reported two bills for the consideration of each house. On the 25th January, that of Mr. Robbins* was taken up in the Senate, and, after an animated discussion, laid on the table by a vote of 20 to 15. Mr. Adams made the report before referred to to the other house; but no action was taken thereon; and no decisive action by either branch took place until the 9th January, 1845, when the Senate again had the subject before them, upon a bill reported by Mr. Tappan on the 6th of June, 1844, and an interesting discussion took place—Senators Tappan, Choate, Woodbury, Buchanan, Crittenden, and Rives taking part.† Mr. Tappan's bill proposed to found at Washington an institution to teach the scientific principles of certain useful arts, and to appoint, on permanent salaries, a professor of agriculture, horticulture, and rural economy; professors of natural history, of chemistry, geology, astronomy, architecture and domestic science, together with occasional auxiliary lectures—all those professors and lecturers "to have special reference in all their illustrations and instructions to the productive and liberal arts of life—to improvements in agriculture, manufactures, trades, and domestic economy"—to analyze different kinds of soils, and to learn and teach how to enrich them—illustrate the working of mines—to teach navigation—to illustrate the theory and practice of building, lighting, and ventilating all manner of edifices—to make experiments to see what exotics will and what will not grow in the United States. No books to be purchased for the institution "except works on science and arts, especially such as relate to the ordinary business of life, and to the various mechanical and other improvements and discoveries which may be made."

* Senate bill No. 293.

† See report in Cong. Globe, January 10, 1845; National Intelligencer, January 11, 12, 24, 1845.

A principal objection urged against this was that the ground was already occupied by more than 173 colleges, which would sooner or later furnish all the facilities here proposed; but Mr. Tappan contended that the effect and object of the bill was to establish something like the Garden of Plants in Paris, to which we had nothing analogous in this country. Mr. Smithson had passed a great part of the last years of his life in this garden, and Mr. T. was impressed with the idea that, in making this bequest, he had in view the establishment of such a garden in Washington. In this opinion, as to Smithson's intentions, Mr. Woodbury concurred, but thought the permanent professorships should be left out, and provision made for lectures by the most able men who could be employed from time to time. He also favored a more liberal allowance to the library, and vesting the management in the National Institution, an incorporated society in the District. Mr. Rives thought if men were to go to Paris for a model, the lectures at the Sorbonne (*Facultè des Lettres*) would furnish a system more nearly in accordance with the words of the bequest. Mr. Choate, Mr. Pearce, and others, advocated the appropriation of a large portion of the funds to a great library, and gave some curious statistics as to the wants of the country in this respect.

While the numerous colleges of the country were well provided with instruction in most of the departments, they all called for more books for their libraries, and one great library of reference was wanted at some convenient place. Of all the printed books in the world, it was doubtful if we had in this country more than 50,000 different works.

Most of our great writers had been obliged to go to Europe to consult books. The Congressional Library, though improving constantly, was in theory a library to furnish Congress with the means of doing their official business, and members must be allowed to take them to their rooms. So of the libraries in the Departments. They were needed for officials in the daily course of business, and none of these could be opened to the student with the advantages which the Smithsonian library, of books to be constantly retained in the room, would afford.

With such an aid, said Mr. Choate, "our learned men would grow more learned and able; our studies deeper and wider; our mind itself exercised and sharpened; the whole culture of the community raised and enriched. This is, indeed, the increase and diffusion of knowledge." * * "Not among the principal, nor yet the least of reasons for doing so, is that all the while that you are laying out your money, and when you have laid it out, you have the money's worth, the value received, the property purchased on hand, to show for itself and to speak for itself."

"Another reason, not the strongest to be sure, for this mode of expenditure, is that it creates so few jobs and sinecures."

Such considerations as these led to the amendment of the bill on Mr. Choate's motion, so as to leave out all the professorships, reserving the provision for lectures, botanic garden, laboratory, &c., and directing $20,000 of the annual income to be invested in a library, without restriction as to the kind of books. It passed the Senate, January 23d, 1845, but was not reached in the House.

On the 28th February, 1846, Mr. Robert Dale Owen, from the select committee in the House to which the Senate bill had been referred, reported a substitute, which was taken up for consideration on the 22d April, 1846.

This substitute resembled Mr. Tappan's bill in many respects, differing from it mainly in an additional provision for a Normal school, or school for teachers.

We will take this occasion to say, that great credit is due to Mr. Owen for his perseverance in urging upon the House the importance of decided action in disposing of this bequest. No one did more to press it to a vote, and thus redeem the country from any imputation of violating plighted faith. His proposition for a Normal school, which, however, he did not urge very strenuously, met with no favor. His speech is an interesting review of the various plans which had previously been presented, and with a reply to Mr. Choate's argument in favor of large appropriations for a library. He was answered, mainly on the latter topic, by Mr. Marsh, of Vermont, in an excellent speech.

A most extraordinary motion was made by Mr. G. W. Jones, of Tennessee, to amend by a provision that the fund should be paid over to the heirs-at-law of James Smithson, *not in money, but in the worthless Arkansas stock.* Whatever may be said about the impropriety of holding a trustee liable for investments made in good faith, such a proposition made on behalf of a Government which had pledged its faith to carry into effect the objects of the testator, is too evidently contemptible to merit comment; but the fact that the proposition was made is worthy of note, as showing to what extremes some men will go.

Mr. Simms, of South Carolina, moved to return the principal, with interest, in money, to the Court of Chancery in England, believing its acceptance to have been unconstitutional. Mr. Adams took the ground in contradiction to that assumed in some of his previous reports, that, before taking any action on the subject, Congress should wait until Arkansas paid up. Mr. Morse, of Louisiana, proposed a plan for offering rewards for the best original dissertations on science and art, which was, with the previous amendments, voted down. Finally, Mr.

Hough, of New York, brought forward a substitute for the whole bill, to which Mr. Marsh offered several amendments, *with a view, as he said, to direct the appropriation entirely to the purposes of a library,* all of which were adopted. Among these amendments was one striking out two sections of Mr. Hough's bill, *which sections directed the Regents to cause to be printed, from time to time, any lecture or lectures, essays, pamphlets, magazines, or other brief works for diffusing information among the people.* Thus amended, the bill was passed, and sent to the Senate, where it was reported with amendments by Mr. Dix, of New York, but it would have failed for want of attention only, had not Mr. Evans, of Maine, on the last day of the session, urged upon the Senate the importance of disposing of the subject, when it was immediately passed as it came from the House, and the necessary Regents appointed.

Thus, on the tenth day of August, 1846, eight years after receiving the money, Congress redeemed its pledged faith in this matter.

We have presented the foregoing rapid sketch of the various movements in reference to this subject, in order to give some idea of the number of minds which have at different times been engaged upon it, and to aid, if possible, in determining what plan best represented the views of the majority of thinking men.

By this charter, as by all others that were proposed, the whole original fund was loaned to the United States Treasury from the date of its reception, in 1838, at six per cent. interest, the principal to remain unimpaired, and the interest to be appropriated to the maintenance of the institution. (§ 2.)

The immediate government is vested in a Board of Regents, consisting of the Vice President and Chief Justice of the United States, the Mayor of Washington, three Members of the Senate, and three of the House of Representatives, appointed by the presiding officers, and six citizens at large, to be appointed by Congress. The Regents to be paid necessary travelling expenses, five to constitute a quorum. (§ 3.)

"The Smithsonian Institution" *proper*, or "establishment for the increase and diffusion of knowledge among men," to consist of a supervisory or visitorial board, composed of the ex-officio members, not in Congress, of the Board of Regents, with the addition of the President of the United States, the Heads of Departments, except the Interior, (since organised,) and the Commissioner of Patents, and such other persons as they may elect honorary members, who are to have perpetual succession, &c. (§ 1.)

This body is authorized to hold such meetings for the supervision of the affairs of the institution, and the advice and instruction of the

Board of Regents as may be provided for by the by-laws, at which the President, and in his absence the Vice President, shall preside. (§ 8.)

The officers to consist of a Chancellor, who is to preside over the Board of Regents, and a Secretary who shall be secretary to "the Institution" and the Regents, and shall call a meeting on the application of any three; (§ 3;) who shall take charge of the building and property of the institution, keep records of proceedings, &c., and may, with consent of Regents, employ assistants. (§ 7.)

The Regents to select a site for a building to be erected, either so as to form a wing of the Patent Office building, or on any other convenient part of the public grounds, to be of plain and durable materials and structure, without unnecessary ornament, and of sufficient size, and with suitable rooms or halls for the reception and arrangement, upon a liberal scale, of objects of natural history, including a geological and mineralogical cabinet; also a chemical laboratory, a library, a gallery of art, and the necessary lecture rooms. (§§ 4 and 5.)

In proportion as suitable arrangements can be made for their reception, all objects of art, and of foreign and curious research, objects of natural history, plants, and geological and mineralogical specimens, in Washington, belonging to the United States, to be transferred to such persons as the Regents may appoint to receive them, and placed by him in the building under custody of the Regents, who are authorized to make exchanges. Smithson's effects to be preserved separate and apart from all other property. (§ 6.)

The Regents to make, from the interest, an appropriation, not exceeding an average of twenty-five thousand dollars annually, for the gradual formation of a library composed of valuable works pertaining to all departments of human knowledge. (§ 8.)

Of any other moneys not herein appropriated, or not required for the purposes herein provided, the managers are authorized to make such disposal as they shall deem best suited for the promotion of the purpose of the testator, any thing herein contained to the contrary notwithstanding. (§ 9.)

One copy of every copy-right work shall, within three months from publication, be deposited in the library. (§ 10.)

Congress to have the right of repealing, altering, or amending, contracts not being impaired. (§ 11.)

It will be seen that the act requires that there be provided a hall or halls for a museum, a chemical laboratory, necessary lecture rooms, and a gallery of art.

They render necessary an annual appropriation to collect and support li brary, another to maintain a museum; and indicate an intention that a portion of the annual interest should be applied to the advancement of physical science and arts, in part by lectures. This part of the act may be appropriately referred to as the SPECIFIED OBJECTS.

But, after enumerating these items, the framers of the charter added a clause, authorizing the Board, as to all funds *not herein appropriated or not required for the purposes specified*, to make "such disposal as they shall deem best suited for the promotion of the purpose of the testator." The expenditures under this head, we will designate as GENERAL OPERATIONS. The words we have italicised suggested a question which was the subject of much discussion in the Board of Regents—*what funds are required "for purposes herein provided?"* How far is the act to be considered as intimating the opinion of Congress, on the true construction of Smithson's will, and consequently to govern the Regents? Is the provision, for instance, that a sum *not exceeding* twenty-five thousand dollars shall be annually expended on a library to be regarded as binding the Board to make, in the outset, large appropriations to that object, or, will an expenditure of one or two thousand dollars a year be a sufficient compliance? As indicative of the first impressions on this point, we may here mention that the Board, soon after organizing, resolved, that for the present $20,000 should be appropriated for the purchase of books, and fitting up of a library, to commence from January 1st, 1848, a resolution which was never carried into effect, it being urged that it was repealed by the subsequent action of the Board. The first Board of Regents was composed of a number of those who had taken interest in the subject from the commencement. They were Vice President Dallas, Chief Justice Taney, Mayor Seaton, Senators Evans, Cass, and Breese, Representatives Owen, Hough, and Hilliard, Rufus Choate, Richard Rush, Gideon Hawley, W. C. Preston, Professor A. D. Bache, and Col. J. G. Totten. Mr. Dallas was elected Chancellor, and, in his address on laying the corner-stone, thus alluded to the discussions: "How best to put this Smithsonian Institution in progress; to give it definite character and views; to shape its line of march as Congress has either ordered or intimated that it should be, and to let the testamentary purpose be apparent in all its operations, was a task on which ability and much consultation have been expended. There was—I may almost say—necessarily, and of course there was on this cardinal point, great diversity of sentiment and construction, as there had been during the masterly debates which prefaced the passage of the law. What constituted "*knowledge*" in the sense of Smithson's bequest? In what manner shall its "*increase*" be provided for? By what methods shall its "*diffusion*" be sought? Should the developments of the laboratory be more engrossing than the stored resources of the library? Will oral expositions or printed treatises be preferable? Are permanent professorships to be systematized, or temporary teachers to be enlisted? In fine, what should be the instruments and the orbit of an establishment whence the light of knowledge was required constantly to radiate among men.

"They to whom was confided the resolution of these problems into practical measures, have felt the weight and delicacy of their mission. They began by profoundly studying the subject in its several aspects. They cherished with ardor, and discussed with freedom their respective projects. The conflicts of upright minds, however, rarely fail to end in mutual concession and compromise; and thus scarcely a single measure was adopted except by unanimous concurrence." The discussions in the Board were not public; but as near as we have been able to gather, the following is a correct outline of the leading views presented:

It was contended on the one side, that one of the specified objects alone, the care of the Government museum, would absorb a large portion of their income, and leave little or nothing for the others; so with regard to the library, an appropriation anywhere near the limit fixed, would absorb all their resources; a result which the framers of the act could not have intended; and all they meant to require was, that accommodations should be provided for all specified objects on a liberal scale, and this, in deference to the future rather than the present, since a library, museum, and gallery of art were almost certain to grow up along with any literary or scientific establishment, in course of time; and the Government had only placed the national collections at their disposal, in case the Regents thought fit to appoint any officer to receive them. That the "establishment" named in the first and eighth sections, was, with its honorary members, intended for a learned society, to supervise and direct the operations of the Regents; and, it was absurd to suppose that this society was constituted simply to look after the specified objects; but if regarded in connection with the idea of a reasonable discretion being vested in the Regents, as to the time and manner of securing the library, museum, and gallery of art, and the kind of lectures to be delivered, the whole act seemed to be harmonious; that such a construction would best accomplish the intentions of the testator as expressed in his will, quoted in the first section of the act, and to carry out which intentions was the object aimed at by the framers, in expressly leaving a discretion to the Regents by the ninth section. It could not be supposed that they intended to postpone the operations of this section until all the specified objects should be provided for; because that would also be suspending the operations of the visitorial power, or, at all events, make it merely nominal for a long period; that the subjects specified in the act, with the exception of the chemical laboratory, had reference, almost exclusively, to the diffusion of knowledge. That if they were to establish professorships and courses of lectures, with libraries, &c., they would only be multiplying the means of instruction and stimulants to exertion which were already possessed by other institutions of the land. It was desirable to devise some plan which would not interfere with, but, as far as possible, secure the coöperation of all other institutions. That the interest with which the libraries and cabinets of London and Paris are thronged by students and savans was in no small degree to be attributed to the influence of those establishments which encourage effort in every department, either by the prospect of direct rewards, or the honors and privileges of membership. That, in the United States, the great drawback to original research was more the want of sufficient stimulus than the absence of facilities in the way of libraries and apparatus, imperfect as these ordinarily were. Most of those who possessed inclination and ability, either had not the leisure from other occupations, or were discouraged by the apparent lack of interest of those about them. They therefore proposed, as a more practical way of increasing and diffusing knowledge, to offer suitable rewards for memoirs containing new truths, and appropriate, annually, a portion of the income for particular researches under the direction of suitable persons, and for publishing, periodically, reports on the progress of the different branches of knowledge, and occasionally, separate treatises on subjects of general interest. That as to judges, there could be no reason to apprehend any difficulty in enlisting the support of all men of scientific learning in the country, and though the main security against abuse must be in the sound judgment of the officers having charge, yet the danger of wasting money here was not greater than in collecting a vast mass of useless lumber and curious trinkets in the museum; that such publications and investigations would make the Institution well known every where, and secure valuable books and other articles in exchange.

That there might be some spirit of opposition engendered in the breasts of those who were competitors for the prizes or honors might readily be believed. But the names of unsuccessful aspirants could be concealed from those who decide upon their productions, as well as from the public; and the constant changes which would take place in the *ex officio* members of the Institution would be sufficient security against any one set of views or of prejudices obtaining an undue supremacy for any great length of time.

On the other side it was contended that the specified objects were chiefly regarded by the charter, and that the Board were bound first to apply all the income to those objects which were expressly named, until they should be so far perfected that the annual appropriations for each purpose might be lessened, and thus a surplus be acquired, which could be applied, under the discretionary clause, to general operations—that this was not only the most obvious, but the safest interpretation to put upon the law, since a large collection of the materials of knowledge is certain, in the long run, to lead to research and publication to a greater or less extent; and is less liable to abuse than any scheme which mainly depends upon the management and judgment of those who control it; that such collections tend to *increase* as well as to *diffuse* knowledge, for, in proportion as the materials for study are accumulated, a stimulus and facility is furnished for research, and consequently for study and invention. That the action of Congress upon the proposition of Mr. Morse, and the whole tenor of the debates, indicated that any scheme of publications was not favored, that it would lead to the expenditure of money upon unworthy objects, or upon those which do not stand in need of such aid, and which would, without it, be brought before the public through the medium of scientific journals or of private enterprise. No class of men adhere more tenaciously to their opinions, or are more jealous of others than those who think they have made new discoveries; and every rejected memorial would embitter the feelings of the disappointed party, and thus the Institution be exposed to continual attacks, and be building up for itself a strong opposing party. If the judges chanced to be incompetent, or were without any strong stimulus to the proper fulfilment of their tasks, memoirs would be accepted which were not in reality additions to knowledge, and thus lower the character of the Institution and prevent its papers being read. There were very few writers, it was said, who could not find the means of publication if their works really contained anything that was worthy of it. It was further objected, that the whole success of the scheme would depend upon its management; and, if at any time one incompetent secretary should be elected, he might render the whole system an outlet for the visionary speculations of dabblers in science and literature. And this would, more especially, be the case with regard to the second branch of the plan for increasing knowledge; to wit, the institution of definite lines of research, scarcely one of which would not in the end exceed in expense the original calculation, as is the case with all such schemes when entered into by Congress.

That, though the Board of Regents and the visitors would undoubtedly interfere when glaring abuses became apparent, yet, constitnted as these bodies were, mostly of persons holding other official positions, or actively engaged in other pursuits away from Washington, and meeting only at long intervals, they could not be expected to exercise a very close supervision over the ordinary transactions—hence the necessity of regulating the discretion of the officers by strict bounds.

That, as the library was the only specified object in connection with which the act named any sum, it was a fair construction to conclude that this was a principal mode intended by Congress; and that the gradual formation of a universal library, equal to the first class libraries of the old world, was more needed in this country than any other instrumentality; since our scholars, after having pursued their researches as far as possible at home, could go to Washington for a few weeks, to continue and perfect their acquirements, and distribute the results by the thousand voices of the press throughout the world; they would come to Washington, as they now go to Germany. And, after all this should be accomplished, the fund would remain unimpaired for future objects, suggested, stimulated, and rendered practicable by the resources and facilities furnished by this great central storehouse of intellectual treasures.

After a vast amount of discussion to this effect, a compromise was made between conflicting opinions, by agreeing to divide the income into two equal parts. One part to be appropriated to general operations, or publications and researches; the other part to the specified objects, or library, museum, &c. The details for the management of each of these departments are given in a programme presented in the first annual report of the Secretary, and adopted by the Board, December 13, 1847, from which we extract some leading views:

"A library will be required, consisting, 1st, of a complete collection of the transactions and proceedings of all the learned societies in the world; 2d, of the more important current periodical publications, and other works necessary in preparing the periodical reports.

"The institution should make special collections, particularly of objects to illustrate and verify its own publications.

"Also, a collection of instruments of research in all branches of experimental science.

"With reference to the collection of books, other than those mentioned above, catalogues of all the different libraries in the United States should be procured, in order that the valuable books first purchased may be such as are not to be found in the United States.

"Also, catalogues of memoirs, and of books in foreign libraries, and other materials, should be collected for rendering the Institution a centre of bibliographical knowledge, whence the student may be directed to any work which he may require.

"It is believed that the collections in natural history will increase by donation as rapidly as the income of the Institution can make provision for their reception, and, therefore, it will seldom be necessary to purchase articles of this kind.

"Attempts should be made to procure for the gallery of arts casts of the most celebrated articles of ancient and modern sculpture.

"The arts may be encouraged by providing a room, free of expense, for the exhibition of the objects of the Art-Union and other similar societies.

"A small appropriation should annually be made for models of antiquities, such as those of the remains of ancient temples, &c.

"The duty of the Secretary will be the general superintendence, with the advice of the Chancellor and other members of the establishment, of the literary and scientific operations of the Institution; to give to the Regents annually an account of all the transactions; of the memoirs which have been received for publication; of the researches which have been made; and to edit, with the assistance of the librarian, the publications of the Institution.

"The duty of the Assistant Secretary, acting as librarian, will be, for the present, to assist in taking charge of the collections, to select and purchase, under the direction of the Secretary and a committee of the board, books and catalogues, and to procure the information before mentioned; to give information on plans of libraries, and to assist the Secretary in editing the publications of the Institution, and in the other duties of his office.

"The publications to consist of, 1st, "SMITHSONIAN CONTRIBUTIONS," consisting of the works elicited by rewards offered to men of talents for memoirs containing new truths; and the results of particular researches made by direction of the Institution. 2d, "SMITHSONIAN REPORTS," consisting of reports on the progress of knowledge. The first to aid the *increase*, the latter, to aid the *diffusion* of knowledge.

"The Secretary and his assistants, during the session of Congress, will be required to illustrate new discoveries in science, and to exhibit new objects of art; distinguished individuals should also be invited to give lectures on subjects of general interest."

The Secretary, in his recent reports, declares that an attempt has been made in good faith to carry out this arrangement for division of the income, so far as that income has been applied to the general support of the Institution; and that, if items which may be properly charged to the library and collections were added to this side of the account, the balance would be in favor of the general—or, as he styles them, "active" operations. But, he declares that the plan has not been found to work well in practice; that the income is too small to properly support more than one system of operations; and that, therefore, the attempt to sustain three departments, with separate ends and separate interests, must lead to inharmonious action, and, consequently, to diminished usefulness; that, however proper such a division of the income might have been in the beginning, in order to harmonize conflicting opinions, and to submit with proper caution the several proposed schemes to a judicious trial, the same considerations do not exist for its continuance, changes having occurred which materially alter the conditions on which it was founded; that the plan of general or "active" operations was not at first fully understood, even by the literary men of the country, it being considered chimerical, and incapable of being continued for any length of time; and hence it was thought important to provide for the means of falling back upon a library and collections; that the experience of six years has, however, established its practicability and importance, and it is now considered, by the great majority of intelligent persons who have studied the subject, the only direct means of realizing the intention of the donor. That the building was to have been finished in five years, and the income after this was to be increased by the interest on the remaining surplus fund; but the Regents have found it necessary for the better security of the library and museum to add fifty thousand dollars to the cost of the edifice; and ten years will have elapsed from the beginning, instead of five, before any income from the surplus fund wi'l be available. That this additional expense is not incurred for the "active" operations, and the question may be asked, whether they ought to bear any part of this additional burden.

It should here be explained, that by a resolution of the Board, the amount of accrued interest ($242,129) at the time of organization, which by the act was appropriated to the building, was drawn from the treasury and invested at interest, and by deferring the completion of the building and investing from time to time portions of the annual income, there has been laid aside a sum of upwards of $200,000, notwithstanding that the edifice will have cost when completed $300,000. The amount thus laid aside it is proposed to add to the principal of $500,000, thus increasing the annual income proportionally.

The Secretary goes on to remark, in substance, that the inquiry may be made, whether it is advisable in the present state of the funds, and the wants of the "active" operations, to expend any considerable portion of the income in the reproduction of a collection of objects of nature and art. Again: the active operations are procuring annually for the library, by exchange, a large number of valuable books, which, in time, of themselves will form a rare and valuable collection, and, even if the division of the income is to be continued, a sum equal in amount to the price of these books ought to be charged to the library, and an equal amount credited to the "active" operations. That, though a large library connected with the Institution would be valuable in itself, and convenient to those who are in the immediate vicinity of the Smithsonion building, yet, as has been said before, it is not essentially necessary to the active operations. It would be of comparatively little importance to the greater number of the co-laborers of the Institution, who are found in every part of the United States, and are not confined even to these limits. But few of the authors of the Smithsonian memoirs reside in Washington. The libraries, therefore, of the whole country, and in some cases of other countries, are at the service of the Institution, and employed for its purposes. That, with regard to the museum, it is not the intention of the Institution to attempt to examine and describe within the walls of its own building all the objects which may be referred to it. To accomplish this, a corps of naturalists, each learned in his own branch, would be required, at an expense which the whole income would be inadequate to meet. That the more feasible and far less expensive organization was adopted, of referring all scientific questions of importance, as well as objects of natural history, for investigation, to persons of reputation and learning in different parts of the United States, and perhaps, in some cases in foreign countries. By the operation of this plan, which has been found eminently practicable, the collections, as well as the libraries of the whole country, are rendered subservient to the use of the Institution. That there can be but little doubt that, in due time, ample provision will be made for a library and museum at the capital of this Union worthy of a government whose perpetuity depends upon the virtue and intelligence of the people. It is, therefore, unwise in his opinion, to hamper the more important objects of this Institution, by attempting to anticipate results which will be eventually produced without the expenditure of its means.

It not being any part of our plan to give more than an outline of the history of the Institution for the information of the general reader, we shall not enter into an elaborate discussion as to the correctness of this reasoning of the Secretary. It is understood that a difference of opinion exists among those who have had the best opportunities to examine, as to whether the compromise has been fairly tried, and justice done, as far as the means would allow, to each department. To decide on this point, and also as to the merits of the general or "active" operations, involves the necessity of examining very carefully all the proceedings of the Board of Regents and their accounts; and also the publications of the Institution, with the aid of superior knowledge and experience, in order to determine whether they are positive additions to knowledge, and if so, whether the results, however new or curious, are of a value proportionate to the cost; and further, whether the substance of most, if not all of them, might not have been brought before the world through other agencies to quite as much advantage for science, if not in quite so elegant a form.

Admitting, however, that the "active" operations have accomplished all that is claimed by the Secretary, are his conclusions correct as to there being necessarily any want of harmony in action between this department and the specified objects? Are the ends and interests necessarily separate? Do not the short reports of the assistants, which are embodied in the reports to the Regents, show that those having charge of the library and collections of natural history, even with limited aid, have gathered valuable information from what has come to their knowledge in organizing their departments; and is there no reason to suppose that from these quarters some of the best contributions to knowledge may, in time, emanate? It may be true that the Library of Congress and the collections of Government will save the necessity of as large an expenditure in the first instance as might have been otherwise advisable; but this only shows the propriety of more care and discrimination in purchasing for the Institution; and the value of the Government collections will be the greater in proportion as the officers in charge of those at the Smithsonian, are intelligent and capable of distinguishing what is new and useful, and giving the results to the world, either through their annual reports, or through the more imposing volumes of "contributions" or "reports."

The principal difficulty adverted to by the Secretary, is the want of sufficient annual income for all. Hence he infers the necessity of confining the expenditures mainly to one department. Is not the alternative rather a reduction of all the expenditures in each department, and thereby continuing to add every year to the income? If the income is, say $40,000 per annum, why may not the expeditures be so limited as to add every year $10,000, to the principal, and thus add at least six hundred dollars a year to the income. The development of the Institution would not in this way be perhaps quite as rapid as if the whole expenditure were confined to one department; but, in course of time, each would become well endowed.

We confess, however, that we have never been entirely satisfied that the Regents had the power to increase their capital by this means. The act expressly appropriated $242,129 to the building, and if the Regents had the power to postpone the application of it to that purpose for eight years, why could they not have postponed it indefinitely? So the income of about $30,000 was expressly appropriated to the support of the Institution—and if a portion of that could be added to the capital, why not postpone any operations whatever, until the capital was sufficiently large? Had Congress thought this course best, they might have delayed the establishment of the Institution twenty years instead of ten. But, if the course pursued by the Regents is proper, surely it is right that the objects expressly named in the act should have the benefit of it.

In this connection it is proper to advert to the fact that the Institution has received a valuable donation of chemical and philosophical apparatus from Professor Hare, of Philadelphia, (now one of the honorary members,) and has become the contingent legatee of the sum of $75,000, from Mr. Wynn, of Brooklyn, New York, who has left this amount to the Institution, on the death without issue of his daughter, now a child six years old. In making this bequest, the testator says in his will, "I know no benevolent Institution more useful and appropriate than the Smithsonian Institution at Washington." "This circumstance," says the Secretary, "is highly gratifying to the friends of the Institution, not because it offers a remote possibility of an increase of the funds, but on account of the evidence it affords of the liberal views of the deceased, and of his confidence in the proper management and importance of the Smithsonian bequest. The will of Mr. Wynn induces us to believe that the right administration of the Smithsonian fund will cause similar examples of liberality on the part of wealthy individuals of our country; and in this point of view the responsibility which rests on those who have the direction of the affairs of this Institution is greater than that with reference to the good which the income itself may immediately accomplish. Though it is scarcely to be expected that many unconditional bequests will be made, yet the example of Smithson may induce the founding of other institutions which may serve to perpetuate other names, and increase the blessings which may flow from such judicious liberality. Man is a sympathetic being; and it is not impossible that Smithson himself may have caught the first idea of his benevolent design from the example of our countryman, Count Rumford, the principal founder of the Royal Institution of London. Bequests for special purposes, bearing the names of the testators, are not incongruous with the plan of this Institution. Lectureships on particular subjects, annual reports on special branches of knowledge, provision for certain lines of research, and libraries for general use or special reference, may be founded under the names of those who bestow the funds, and be placed under the direction of, and incorporated with, the Smithsonian Institution."

Having the utmost confidence that, in reference to the changes proposed by the Secretary, the intelligence and sound judgment of those having its government in charge, will ultimately lead to correct conclusions, we will only add one or two remarks.

First, with reference to the benefit to be derived to the city of Washington from the location of the Institution, upon which so much stress was laid in the Senate when the object was first introduced into that body. It must be obvious, on a moment's reflection, that in proportion as the establishment gains a reputation throughout the country by its usefulness in the increase and diffusion of knowledge, in the same proportion will it attract visitors and students to the capital;

and the question is, what will best accomplish this, a larger collection here of the materials for study than is to be found elsewhere, or the printing of learned contributions, or both?

Secondly, in forming an opinion on this point, it is hardly to the purpose to speculate upon Smithson's intentions as indicated by his habits of life, studies, and associations. It is extremely doubtful whether he had any very definite idea of what he wished to create; if he had, there seems to be no reason why he should have not more fully explained his wishes, as the will was apparently not made when he thought himself in *extremis*; and he had time enough between the date of it and his death to have perfected it in this respect. He had, probably, like most great students, learned so much as to sensibly appreciate his own ignorance of the vast field yet before him, and distrusted his own power to mark out a plan which would answer for all time to come, and not embarrass the trustees in its fulfillment. Reasoning thus, and perhaps thinking it would hardly be respectful to the nation whom he constituted trustees, to mark, and too closely, any course they were to pursue, preferred to leave the whole subject to the judgment of the men of experience who would be called to act upon the matter.

And in this last connection, resuming the course of our narrative, we will state that but two or three meetings have been held of the visitorial Board, who are to constitute the Smithsonian Institution proper. At these meetings they have done little more than elect honorary members, but manifested a disposition to admit no one to that position who had not already obtained distinction and influence in the world of letters and science; and if suitable regulations are adopted in this respect, we cannot but hope that, in course of time, an interest may be created in the Institution which would exercise a most happy influence in correcting abuses and securing the best system. The great difficulty with most societies for the increase and diffusion of knowledge in this country is, that the privileges of membership are too readily granted, without reference to the qualifications of the candidates, so that the mere fact of being a member of such a society is in itself no evidence of scholarship, and, consequently, of but little value as an honor.

Suppose for example a plan be adopted—

1st. Limiting the number of honorary members to be elected in any one year.

2d. Fixing upon certain qualifications as essential to a nomination for membership; such, for example, as the production of some work, the successful prosecution of some research, or great distinction as an instructor in the higher branches.

3d. Giving to the members thus elected the privilege of receiving copies of all the publications of the Institution during their life time, and of attending all meetings of the Board of Regents.

4th. Recommending to Congress that, whenever vacancies shall occur in the Board of Regents, the vacancy shall, as far as practicable and consistent with the provisions of law on that behalf, be filled from the honorary members. By the first provision, the honor would be more valuable, as being more rare; by the second, it would be made more sure evidence of merit; and the third and fourth, would give it more intrinsic value; the last one securing to the regents men familiar with the course of business, and amply qualified; while the whole would tend eventually to interest in the establishment a number of learned men who would act as counsellors, and who, being familiar with the operations, would always present from their ranks suitable persons to fill the offices. It would be establishing a method of distinguishing men of letters hitherto almost unknown in our country. Probably this would be the means of drawing annually to Washington large numbers of such men, and making the Smithsonian halls the place of annual meeting for the various learned societies, since they might expect, from amongst the honorary members and regents, to find many whose presence and participation in the discussions would add greatly to the interest of their deliberations.

By such an arrangement as this a strong inducement will be offered to writers, independently of the premiums, and the distinction of having their contributions brought before the world with the stamp of authority which a publication in the "Contributions" would give to them; for the position of "honorary member" of the Institution would be invested with some of those attractions which make a membership of the Academy of Science at Paris so much an object of ambition.

Thus the Smithsonian Institution and the city of Washington may be made, in course of time, to occupy the position now held by Philadelphia as the headquarters of original research; especially if the materials of knowledge, in the shape of books, apparatus, and collections, be found there in greater perfection than elsewhere; and from this, as a central point, rays of knowledge will be diffused to all parts of the Union—the accomplishment of which must be, in no small degree, aided by its connection with the Government, and the number of officers in the army and navy, consular agents, and intellectual travellers who will thus be brought within the immediate circle of its influence, advantages which Smithson no doubt had in view in requiring that it should be established at "Washington."

We do not und rtake to describe what has been done either in the general or local operations, as the statements on these subjects change every year, and no condensed account would do justice to the reports of Professors Henry, Jewett, and Baird, contained in the Annual Reports of the Regents, which, being published by Congress, are readily obtained either at the Institution or of any member of Congress.

Suffice it to say, that the library and museum already contain a very respectable collection. A large proportion of both has been made up by donations and exchanges, and experience shows that the increase in this way, especially in the museum, will continue to be very rapid. Indeed, the Institution will soon have so many collections of its own, as to occupy a large proportion of the new building. Except in the purchase of a collection of fine old engravings, there have been no investments in objects of art; but the room intended, though not suited for that purpose, has been occupied for the exhibition of private collections. The lectures have been mostly of a popular kind, and the room always crowded.

The building, which is now nearly completed, has been changed somewhat in its interior arrangements, since Mr. Dallas described it in his corner-stone address. His description of the exterior is probably as accurate as can be given of such a structure.

"Its exterior presents a specimen of the style of architecture that prevailed some six centuries ago, chiefly in Germany, Normandy, and Southern Europe, which preceded the Gothic, and continues to recommend itself, for structures like this, to the most enlightened judgment. It is known as the Norman, or, more strictly speaking, the Lombard style. It harmonizes alike with the extent, the grave uses, and the massive strength of the edifice; it exacts a certain variety in the forms of its parts; and it authorizes any additions that convenience may require, no matter how seemingly irregular they may be.

"It extends east and west, an entire front of four hundred and twenty-six feet, having a central building of fifty by two hundred feet in the clear, inside, with two towers; two wings of unequal fronts; the east one forty-five by seventy-five feet in the clear, inside, with a vestibule and porch attached to it; the west one thirty-four by sixty-five feet in the clear, inside, with a northern semi-circular projection. These wings will be connected with the central building by two ranges sixty feet in length in the clear, inside. It will have a central rear tower, and other towers of different heights, sizes, and characters, two of them placed in the wings. All these numerous towers are essential to arrangements within—as flues, stairways, ventilators, and detached rooms—and are of different heights, varying from sixty to one hundred and fifty feet."

The material is a freestone, of a lilac grey color, drawn from a quarry on the banks of the Chesapeake and Ohio canal, near Seneca creek, and but twenty-three miles from the spot. It is said not to be subject to the objections that exist against the Potomac freestone, of which the central building of the Capitol, the President's House, Treasury, and central Patent Office building are constructed, growing harder by time. The pictures of the edifice are becoming familiar. Portions of the north central front have been to some extent reproduced in the church of the Puritans, and St. George's church, at New York. Perhaps, a better idea may be given, by saying that it is unlike anything else in the country, and that no two parts are like each other—a variety which is rather pleasing to the eye, and which is carried out in the interior, even in the furniture. It certainly has this advantage, that it may be extended in almost any direction, and in almost any style of architecture—Elizabethan, or Gothic, Saracenic, or Egyptian—without impairing its effect. Its effect has been impaired by want of sufficient depth in proportion to its length, and too prominent an exhibition of the roof. With its towers and cloisters, its chapel, (for a picture gallery!) its battlements, and port-holes like crosses, through which the knights templars might have shot their arquebusses, and its refectory, over which the ivy is beginning to creep, it strongly brings to mind the accounts we read of the fortified monasteries of former times. Greenough thus playfully touches upon it, as seen in a stroll by moonlight across the mall:

"Suddenly, as I walked, the dark form of the Smithsonian palace rose between me and the white Capitol, and I stopped. Tower and battlement, and all that mediæval confusion, stamped itself on the halls of Congress, as ink upon paper! Dark on that whiteness—complication on that simplicity! It scared me. Was it a spectacle, or was not I another Rip Van Winkle who had slept too long? It seemed to threaten, it seemed to say, I bide my time! Oh, it was indeed monastic at that hour! * * * * * * * * * * * * *

"On walking round to the south I was much relieved; I could see through and through the building. This was a departure from all that I had seen in the real old turretted fortresses of theology. It was a good omen.

"I am not about to criticise the edifice. I have not quite recovered from my alarm. There is still a certain mystery about those towers and steep belfries that makes me uneasy. This is a practical land. They must be for something. Is no *coup d'etat* lurking there? Can they be merely ornaments, like the tassels to a university cap?—Perhaps they are an allopathic dose administered to that parsimony which so long denied to science where to lay her head—*contraria contrariis curantur!* They must have cost much money.

"'Bosomed high in tufted trees' the Smithsonian college must in itself be hereafter a most picturesque object; the models whence it has been imitated are both 'rich and rare'; the connoiseurs may well 'wonder how the devil it got *there*.'"*

No one indeed who has a particle of poetry in his soul can fail to be impressed with the picturesque appearance of the pile, as approached from Pennsylvania avenue; but, though he may be gratified that there is one such structure to contrast with the Grecian and Roman architecture which prevails in all the other public buildings, some utilitarian notions will come over him as he enters the building and finds it hard to discover any special use for all these towers, cloisters, and connecting ranges, which only divide up the interior into inconvenient rooms, few of them adapted to any special purpose. The main building, however, which was the last finished, is provided with a much more spacious lecture-room than that which was first used in the eastern wing; also, with spacious apartments for the museum and library.

As before remarked, this building will be, probably, soon filled with a museum collected by the Institution. The act of Congress authorises the transfer to it of all the collections in the Patent Office building; and, with a view to this, provided that, if the President, Heads of Departments, and Commissioner of Patents, consented, the Institution might be so constructed as to form, in appearance, a wing of that edifice; but it was thought that the whole of that building would be ultimately required for the Department of the Interior, and the present site presented a decided advantage in admitting of ornamental grounds, and an enlargement in every direction. On account of the expense, and latterly, of the want of accommodations, the Regents have declined to receive the collections of the Government.

It would certainly be desirable, in every point of view, that the National Museum and that of the Smithsonian be connected together, and placed under one supervision. But Congress surely would not desire that a collection, which has been made by the nation at the cost of two or three Smithsonian bequests, should all go to the credit of Smithson and pass under his name? Yet such will be the practical operation of the act, if the National Museum is merged into the Smithsonian Museum. So strikingly did the impropriety of this appear that, when the act was under consideration in Congress, a member moved that the museum part of the building should be

* Memorial of Horatio Greenough by H. T. Tuckerman, page 90.

called "The National Gallery," which would probably have been carried had there not been coupled with it a proviso for placing the gallery under the direction of the "National Institution for the Promotion of Science." But even had this motion prevailed, something more would be necessary. Would it be becoming the dignity and self-respect of the nation that they should be indebted to the bequest of a liberal foreigner for a building in which to preserve the National Museum? Would it not be more proper that the Government should make an appropriation from the public funds for such portions of this edifice as might be used, or such additions as may be necessary, and for the annual support of the museum. This might be called the National Museum, and all the Smithsonian collections could be placed with those of the Government, under the appropriate classification, each being labelled with the name of Smithson. If something like this be done, and the collections of Government and the Institution placed together, there will be greater facility in examining and preserving them all than when, as now, separated, with different curators and systems, and we may perhaps hope that in course of time, something like the Garden of Plants at Paris will surround it; an object which is certainly every way desirable, having in all countries been regarded as a valuable, if not a principal means for increasing and diffusing knowledge.*

Strictly speaking, the Smithsonian is not a *National* Institution; that is to say, it is upon a private foundation, originating entirely in the bequest of an individual, accompanied however by only one condition, that the trustees shall retain it at Washington. But those trustees are the Congress of the United States, who may at any time make any change, except in location, they may deem advisable, better to accomplish the testator's object; a power which they have to some extent transferred to the visitorial Board, which, with the Board of Regents, must always be composed in part of high Executive officers, and members and appointees of Congress; they have done more, given it ground for its buildings, taken charge of its capital, vested in it the exclusive privilege of copy-right, printed its annual reports &c., and there can be no doubt that they will in due time congregate around it such other establishments as seem to bear upon the same general objects. All that is neces-

---

* If the Regents do not feel called upon to take charge of the whole of the Patent Office collection, there are some things which they might place in the grounds around. Such are the copper rock from Lake Superior, the sarcophagus, brought out by Commodore Elliott, now in the dark basement of the Patent Office, (which we presume the National Institute would not object to their taking.) The Indian paintings might be placed in their gallery.

sary to bring this about, is that there should be a good understanding between the officers of the Institution and those of the Patent Office, Observatory, Agricultural Bureau, of Congress Library, and other departments which now are, or soon will grow up, out of the operations of the Government.* Let it be an object of the members and officers of the establishment, to promote an active co-operation between all these departments, each aiding the other, and the Smithsonian will soon form one of a group which will, unitedly, accomplish more for the increase of knowledge in a short time, than any one could do in years. But to accomplish this, there must be a faithful adherence to the requirements of law; for we think that no one who reads the history of the Institution can fail to be impressed with the belief that the members of Congress who passed the bill, and the public at large, throughout the country, will scarcely be satisfied with any scheme which is intended to develope but one idea, through one channel, or depending for its success upon the judgment of any one individual, however eminent.

---

*The Government libraries are, Congress Library, including the Law Library, (in another part of the Capitol,) and the document libraries attached to the two Houses of Congress, the War Department library, the Patent Office library, and that in the Executive Mansion. They are, none of them, of any great importance, except the first, which has been reëstablished, with the advantage of containing nearly all the books of value destroyed by the late fire, in the latest and best editions. It will be many years, however, before, with the present annual appropriation, (about $5,000,) it will be anything like what it should be. It is especially defective in collections of pamphlets and journals which throw so much light on the history of the times, and which are only to be found in large libraries.

The Government collections, other than those in the Capitol, consist,

1st. Of a collection of paintings comprising portraits of Indian Chiefs who have, at different times, visited the capital, mostly painted by C. B. King, and a number of portraits of distinguished personages, by different artists, presented to Government.

2d. A variety of trinkets, swords, guns, &c., presented, at different times, to the President, and Foreign Ministers, and which were deliver- to the Department of State, Government officials not being allowed to receive presents. An amusing chapter might be made on this subject. Sometimes the presents have consisted of Arabian horses, lions, and other live animals. They have been sold, and the proceeds given to charitable institutions. A rich carpet, presented to President Van Buren, is kept rolled up, in a glass case. It had much better be spread as a rug, in the President's east-room, if the moths have left it in a condition to be seen. A bottle of otto of rose, said to be of immense value, and demijohns of rose water, are also carefully preserved. Their sweetness can hardly be said to be "wasted on the desert air," for it is never, publicly at least, uncorked. If it improves by age, Uncle Sam will have a treasure one of these days.

3d. A series of Indian relics, minerals, &c., belonging to a society called the National Institution for the Promotion of Science, which was incorporated by Congress, and intended to occupy a position similar to the Society of Arts, at Paris. For a time there was much interest taken in its proceedings, honorary members were elected, a correspondence invited from all parts of the world; this action, together with the names of government officers connected with it, elicited many replies from Europe; and the principal business, at each meeting, was a recital of the donations received. But the necessity of relying upon annual subscriptions led to the election to the privileges of membership, of all who would pay the annual fee, which lowered the value of the honor, although many of the most learned and scientific took an active part. The funds received were hardly sufficient to pay the freight on articles presented. The meetings are still kept up, with what success we are not informed; but we put down their collections among those of Government, because, we believe in case of dissolution, they go to the United States. Mr. Woodbury and others advocated the plan of placing the Smithsonian bequest under the control of this society, and two of the Regents are required to be members of it.

4th. The collections of the South Sea Exploring Expedition, consisting of a large number of Indian articles, canoes, skins, implements of war, corals, shells, natural mummies, animals, birds, reptiles, and plants.

It is not generally known that everything in this collection which is new, is being explained and described, with the most exquisite illustrations, in the works of the scientific corps of the Exploring Expedition, seven or eight volumes of which have been issued. The number of volumes will probably reach to twenty, and it will be a work worthy of the Government, and, as far as it goes, will equal, if not excel, any other work of a similar description. Unfortunately, Congress only ordered one hundred copies to be printed, out of which Foreign Governments and the States were to be supplied; and this small number has been still further reduced by the destruction of many copies at the burning of the Congress Library. The plates have, we believe, been given to the Smithsonian Institution.

5th. The Patent Office collection of models may, perhaps, be regarded as a species of museum, as it certainly illustrates the progress of invention.

All these collections, except the living plants, are preserved in the Patent Office building, which, with the new wings will, probably, admit of better accommodation than heretofore. The plants are in conservatories in front of the Capitol.

INDEX.

A.

B.

C.

D.

N.

O.

P.

R.

S.

T.

V.

W.

www.ingramcontent.com/pod-product-compliance
Lightning Source LLC
LaVergne TN
LVHW021420110826
845150LV00007B/2011